CLARIFYING COMMON MISTAKES WIDESPREAD AMONG THE MUSLIMS

Shaykh Ṣāliḥ Āl ash-Shaykh

ISBN: 978-1-4675-8230-8

First Edition: Dhul-Ḥijjah 1438 AH / September 2017 CE

Cover Design: Usul Design
Email: info@usuldesign.com

Translator: Rasheed Barbee

Editing & Formatting: Danielle Lebenson al-Amrikiyyah
www.amrikiyyahdesign.com

Publisher's Information:
Authentic Statements Publishing
P.O. Box 15536
Philadelphia, PA 19131
215.382.3382
215.382.3782 – Fax

Store:
5000 Locust St.(Side Entrance)
Philadelphia, PA 19139

Website: www.authenticstatements.com
E-mail: info@authenticstatements.com

Transliteration Table

Consonants

ء	'	د	d	ض	ḍ	ك	k
ب	b	ذ	dh	ط	ṭ	ل	l
ت	t	ر	r	ظ	ẓ	م	m
ث	th	ز	z	ع	'	ن	n
ج	j	س	s	غ	gh	ه	h
ح	ḥ	ش	sh	ف	f	و	w
خ	kh	ص	ṣ	ق	q	ي	y

Vowels

Short	ـَ	a	ـِ	i	ـُ	u
Long	ـَا	ā	ـِي	ī	ـُو	ū
Diphthongs	ـَي	ay/ai	ـَوْ	aw		

Glyphs

ﷺ *Ṣallāllāhu 'alayhi wa sallam* (May Allāh's praise & salutations be upon him)

رضي الله عنه *Raḍiyallāhu 'anhu* (May Allāh be pleased with him)

رضي الله عنهم *Raḍiyallāhu 'anhum* (May Allāh be pleased with them)

رضي الله عنها *Raḍiyallāhu 'anhā* (May Allāh be pleased with her)

رحمه الله *Raḥimahullāh* (May Allāh have mercy on him)

سبحانه وتعالى *Subḥānahu wa-ta'Ālā* (Glorious and Exalted is He)

Contents

[2] Mistakes in 'Aqīdah & Tawḥīd: Minor Shirk

[3] Mistakes Related to Innovations

[4] Mistakes Related to Purification

[5] Mistakes Regarding the Prayer

[6] Mistakes Related to Du'ā'

[7] Mistakes Concerning Jumu'ah (Friday)

[8] Mistakes Related to Zakāh (Charity)

[9] Mistakes Related to Fasting

[10] Mistakes Related to Ḥajj

[11] Mistakes Related to Business Transactions

[12] Common Mistakes Among Men

[13] Corrupters of the Ears & Eyes

[14] Mistakes Related to Travel

[15] Mistakes Related to Keeping the Ties of Kinship

[16] Mistakes Related to Marriage

[17] Mistakes of the Tongue

[18] Mistakes Related to Parties & Gatherings

[19] Mistakes Regarding Men's Clothing

[20] MISTAKES RELATED TO WOMEN'S CLOTHING

[21] IMITATING NON-MUSLIMS

[22] Mistakes Related to Photography

[23] Mistakes Regarding Family

[24] Mistakes Regarding the Home

[25] Mistakes Regarding Food & Drink

[26] Mistakes Related to Funerals

Introduction

In the name of Allāh, the Most Beneficent, the Most Merciful:

I praise my Lord with the best praise. I fulfill my duty to Him out of love, respect, glorification, veneration, devotion and humility. I praise Him with His beautiful names, lofty perfect attributes, and beautiful wise actions. He is deserving of glorification and praise. He is my Lord; I do not worship anyone other than Him. I do not turn towards anyone other than Him. Wherever I turn, I find myself within His favors. I awaken blessed by His favors and I reach the evening in a similar fashion, although I am not deserving of any of this. I am an ignorant slave, but the virtue of Allāh is vast and His blessings are seen. O Allāh, bestow upon me the ability to thank You for the favors you have bestowed upon me and my parents.

I bear witness that nothing has the right to be worshiped except Allāh and I bear witness that Muḥammad is His slave and Messenger.

As to what follows:

Glad tidings for the slave who recognizes the rights of Allāh upon him, thus he magnifies and glorifies Allāh. Glad tidings for the slave who is certain concerning the difference between the Lord Who controls the affairs of the universe and is obeyed as opposed to the needy slave who must obey.

There is no doubt that the slaves—some of the people—are estranged from the path of guidance. Nothing makes the path burdensome except pride hidden in the soul or deception which fills the chest and the limbs.

It is an obligation upon the Muslim to know with absolute certainty that he or she is a slave and not a lord. They must obey their Lord and not stray away from Him. They must glorify Allāh by obeying Him. Therefore, do not abandon what your Lord and Master has commanded you and do not allow Him to see you doing what He has prohibited. Be shy in front of Allāh. View your life as a gateway to the Hereafter. The Muslim should view the worldly life like the sun during the dawn: soon he will not be able to see it. Consequently, he works in this world with actions that will advance him to the pleasure of his Lord and open for him the doors of Paradise.

How easy is what we put forward despite the greatness of what we anticipate! How delighted are the hearts with worship—the obligatory and supererogatory—because they are the reasons for attaining closeness to Allāh! How beautiful is observing patience in avoiding all that Islām prohibits if the end result is seeing the noble Face of Allāh and enjoying bliss by way of this!

As to what follows:

This treatise contains advice and warnings against that which opposes the legislation of Islām. Ignorance concerning the laws of Islām has become widespread. Those who fall into these matters are of two categories:

1) The one who is aware that the legislation of Islām prohibits these matters but he does not take heed. This individual has not made a just estimate of Allāh such as is due to Him, and he does not reflect upon the magnitude of who He is. He does not ponder: Who is his Lord? What is the meaning of servitude which the slave adorns himself with? What is the meaning of lordship and divinity of worship, which are great noble attributes of Allāh?

2) The one who is ignorant of the rulings while he generally loves the Lord and Master. He is not pleased that Allāh should see him engaged in what He is not pleased with. He seeks the gardens and rivers which contain the ultimate pleasure.

It is only an hour of fear that can separate the two groups, a group in Paradise and a group in the blazing Fire. If Allāh wills, this treatise will increase clarity concerning the rights of Allāh upon the slaves and give insight to what must be abandoned in an effort to respect the rights of Allāh. If Allāh wills, it will enlighten the hearts and sharpen the desire to abandon sins and the neglect of Allāh's rights.

The origin of this treatise is a group of issues collected by the brothers; may Allāh make our and their reward Paradise. And those men who work in the affairs of enjoining the good and forbidding the evil—may Allāh raise for them light and extinguish the fire of their enemies—requested that I explain this collection of affairs in a concise manner using simple terms, mentioning the evidences, clarifying the intent, and giving instructions. So I agreed, having love for them and those like them—those who evil keeps awake at night with concern, and those who stay awake preventing evil. Thus, they love to advise the slaves of Allāh, putting forth sincere advice in the path of bringing life to dead hearts and curing the sick hearts. May Allāh aid them and show them what will please them, and safeguard those who enjoin good and forbid evil, however they fluctuate.

These affairs are explained in brief, with a sense of urgency—almost improvising—so that the commoners and people on a middle level can benefit from it. Thus, it was written for them. And for the purpose of benefit, the issues within are numbered. So I ask the scholars and students of knowledge not to blame me for the weakness in editing. Whatever is found in it which is correct, then let them praise Allāh, and whatever they see of shortcomings, let them pardon and overlook.

— *Ṣāliḥ bin 'Abdul 'Azīz bin Muḥammad Āl ash-Shaykh*

1

Mistakes in *'Aqīdah & Tawḥīd*: Major *Shirk*

First: The polytheism that removes the person from the fold of Islām, and some of the categories of major *shirk* (polytheism).

---

1. Seeking help from the dead, supplicating to them, requesting assistance from them, and drawing close to them with any aspect of worship.

This is major *shirk* which removes the person from the fold of Islām. This is based upon the statement of Allāh the Exalted:

﴿ إِيَّاكَ نَعْبُدُ وَإِيَّاكَ نَسْتَعِينُ ﴾

You (alone) we worship, and you (alone) we ask for help.

[Sūrah al-Fātihah 1:5]

The object of worship was mentioned first: "You (alone)" to show that Allāh alone is specified with worship. This is the meaning of the statement of *tawheed:* "Nothing has the right to be worshiped except Allāh."

From the various acts of worship is *du'ā'* (supplication); rather, *du'ā'* is worship. The Prophet ﷺ said:

الدُّعَاءُ هُوَ الْعِبَادَةُ.

"*Du'ā'* (supplication) is worship."[1]

Giving any aspect of worship to other than Allāh is polytheism and disbelief (*shirk* and *kufr*). Allāh the Exalted said:

﴿ وَمَن يَدْعُ مَعَ اللَّهِ إِلَٰهًا آخَرَ لَا بُرْهَانَ لَهُ بِهِ فَإِنَّمَا حِسَابُهُ عِندَ رَبِّهِ ۚ إِنَّهُ لَا يُفْلِحُ الْكَافِرُونَ ﴾

And whoever invokes (or worships), besides Allāh, any other god, of whom he has no proof, then his reckoning is only with his Lord. Surely! The disbelievers will not be successful.

[Sūrah al-Mu'minūn 23:117]

The word "whoever" is general, thus it comprises everyone to whom it is applicable. Therefore, it is apparent that whoever supplicates to anyone other than Allāh—regardless of who it is—then he is a disbeliever. Allāh the Exalted said:

﴿ وَأَنَّ الْمَسَاجِدَ لِلَّهِ فَلَا تَدْعُوا مَعَ اللَّهِ أَحَدًا ﴾

And verily the *masājid* are for Allāh (alone), so invoke not anyone along with Allāh.

[Sūrah al-Jinn 72:18]

And He said:

﴿ وَقَالَ الْمَسِيحُ يَا بَنِي إِسْرَائِيلَ اعْبُدُوا اللَّهَ رَبِّي وَرَبَّكُمْ ۖ إِنَّهُ مَن يُشْرِكْ بِاللَّهِ فَقَدْ حَرَّمَ اللَّهُ عَلَيْهِ الْجَنَّةَ وَمَأْوَاهُ النَّارُ

[1] Narrated by Nu'man bin Basheer; collected in *Jāmi' at-Tirmidhī* (3555).

﴿ وَمَا لِلظَّالِمِينَ مِنْ أَنصَارٍ ﴾

But the Messiah (Jesus) said: "O Children of Israel! Worship Allāh, my Lord and your Lord." Verily, whosoever sets up partners in worship with Allāh, then Allāh has forbidden Paradise for him, and the Fire will be his abode. And for the wrongdoers there are no helpers.

[Sūrah al-Mā'idah 5:72]

Included in the types of *du'ā'* is making requests, such as requesting rain, seeking help, seeking assistance, and other than that.

---

2. Seeking intercession from the dead is major *shirk.*

This is based upon the statement of Allāh the Exalted:

﴿ أَمِ اتَّخَذُوا مِن دُونِ اللَّهِ شُفَعَاءَ ۚ قُلْ أَوَلَوْ كَانُوا لَا يَمْلِكُونَ شَيْئًا وَلَا يَعْقِلُونَ ﴿٤٣﴾ قُل لِّلَّهِ الشَّفَاعَةُ جَمِيعًا ﴿٤٤﴾ ﴾

Have they taken others as intercessors besides Allāh? Say: "Even if they have power over nothing whatever and have no intelligence?" Say: "To Allāh belongs all intercession."

[Sūrah az-Zumar 39:43-44]

And Allāh ﷻ said:

﴿ وَأَنذِرْ بِهِ الَّذِينَ يَخَافُونَ أَن يُحْشَرُوا إِلَىٰ رَبِّهِمْ ۙ لَيْسَ لَهُم مِّن دُونِهِ وَلِيٌّ وَلَا شَفِيعٌ لَّعَلَّهُمْ يَتَّقُونَ ﴾

And warn therewith (the Qur'ān) those who fear that they will be gathered before their Lord, when there will be neither a protector nor an intercessor for them besides Him, so that they may fear Allāh and keep their duty to Him.

[Sūrah al-An'ām 6:51]

And there are other verses that carry this meaning.

Intercession belongs to Allāh alone, and it is not for anyone other than Allāh to intercede, from those who have died and whose actions have ceased. It is affirmed that seeking intercession and asking other than Allāh, from those who are deceased, is *shirk*. Those most deserving the intercession of the Prophet ﷺ on the Day of Judgment will be the people of *tawheed*, those free from all categories of *shirk*; those who were sincere in their statement that "nothing has the right to be worshiped except Allāh."

---

3. Sacrificing and vowing for the graves, shrines, and deceased is major *shirk*.

As for sacrificing, Allāh the Exalted said:

﴿ قُلْ إِنَّ صَلَاتِي وَنُسُكِي وَمَحْيَايَ وَمَمَاتِي لِلَّهِ رَبِّ الْعَالَمِينَ ﴿١٦٢﴾ لَا شَرِيكَ لَهُ ﴿١٦٣﴾ ﴾

Say (O Muḥammad): "Verily, my prayer, my sacrifice, my living, and my dying are for Allāh, the Lord of all that exists. He has no partner."

[Sūrah al-An'ām 6:162-163]

Just as the prayer is only for Allāh alone, sacrificing—which is to slaughter an animal—is also only for Allāh alone without partners. Allāh said:

﴿ فَصَلِّ لِرَبِّكَ وَانْحَرْ ﴾

Therefore, turn in prayer to your Lord and sacrifice (to Him only).

[Sūrah al-Kawthar 108:2]

Sacrificing:

Sacrificing is from the greatest acts of worship because it involves spilling the blood of an animal sincerely for the sake of Allāh. The person humbles and lowers himself, seeking the reward with Allāh by drawing near to Him with the spilling of the blood of the animal sincerely for Allāh the Exalted. The Prophet ﷺ said:

لَعَنَ اللَّهُ مَنْ ذَبَحَ لِغَيْرِ اللَّهِ.

"Allāh has cursed whoever sacrifices for other than Allāh."[2]

Vowing:

Allāh the Exalted said:

﴿ وَمَا أَنفَقْتُم مِّن نَّفَقَةٍ أَوْ نَذَرْتُم مِّن نَّذْرٍ فَإِنَّ اللَّهَ يَعْلَمُهُ ﴾

And whatever you spend from charity or whatever vow you make, be sure that Allāh knows it all.

[Sūrah al-Baqarah 2:270]

Allāh ﷻ said:

﴿ يُوفُونَ بِالنَّذْرِ وَيَخَافُونَ يَوْمًا كَانَ شَرُّهُ مُسْتَطِيرًا ﴾

They (are those who) fulfill (their) vows, and they fear a Day whose evil will be widespread.

[Sūrah al-Insān 76:7]

This is proof that fulfilling the vows is beloved to Allāh; the person will be rewarded for doing so and it is worship. Consequently, giving any aspect of worship to other than Allāh is *shirk*, as was previously mentioned.

---

[2] Narrated by 'Alī bin Abī Tālib ﷺ; collected in *Ṣaḥīḥ Muslim* (1978).

4. Performing *tawāf* around graves, wiping them, and seeking blessings from them is *shirk.*

Tawāf[3]:

Tawāf is an act of worship, and it is not permissible to perform *tawāf* anywhere other than the Sacred House of Allāh, Masjid al-Harām. This act of worship—*tawāf*—is only performed at the honorable Ka'bah, and likewise the pilgrims walk between Safā' and Marwa[4]. *Tawāf* for other than Allāh is placing worship in its improper place, exalting the graves, resembling the graves to the Sacred House, and performing the act of worship of *tawāf* for other than Allāh.

Wiping the graves and seeking blessings from them:

This is deifying the graves and exalting them, similar to what the pagans used to do with their idols during the Pre-Islamic Days of Ignorance. Anyone who desires to seek blessings from the graves has exalted that which Allāh has not legislated for them to exalt. The proof that this action is *shirk* (polytheism) is the narration of Abū Wāqid al-Laythi. He said:

خَرَجْنَا مَعَ رَسُولِ اللَّهِ صَلَّى اللَّهُ عَلَيْهِ وَسَلَّمَ إِلَى حُنَيْنٍ وَنَحْنُ حَدِيثُو عَهْدٍ بِكُفْرٍ، قَالَ: وَكَانَتْ لِلْكُفَّارِ سِدْرَةٌ يَعْكِفُونَ عِنْدَهَا، وَيَنُوطُونَ بِهَا أَسْلِحَتَهُمْ، يُقَالَ لَهَا ذَاتُ أَنْوَاطٍ، قَالَ: فَمَرَرْنَا بِسِدْرَةٍ فَقُلْنَا: يَا رَسُولَ اللَّهِ، اجْعَلْ لَنَا ذَاتَ أَنْوَاطٍ، فَقَالَ رَسُولُ اللَّهِ صَلَّى اللَّهُ عَلَيْهِ وَسَلَّمَ:

---

[3] **Translator's note:** *Tawāf* refers to the act of worship of walking seven times around the Ka'bah in the Sacred House in Makkah. Allāh said (what can be translated as): "And (remember) when We showed Ibrāhīm the site of the (Sacred) House (saying): 'Associate not anything (in worship) with Me, and sanctify My House for those who circumambulate it, and those who stand up for prayer.'" (Sūrah al-Hajj 22:26)

[4] **Translator's note:** Safā' and Marwah refers to two hills located in the compounds of Masjid al-Harām. Allāh said (what can be translated as): "Verily! As-Safā' and al-Marwah are of the symbols of Allāh." (Sūrah al-Baqarah 2:158)

"اللَّهُ أَكْبَرُ! إِنَّهَا السُّنَنُ، قُلْتُمْ: وَالَّذِي نَفْسِي بِيَدِهِ، كَمَا قَالَ بَنُو إِسْرَائِيلَ
لِمُوسَى: اجْعَلْ لَنَا إِلَهًا كَمَا لَهُمْ آلِهَةٌ قَالَ إِنَّكُمْ قَوْمٌ تَجْهَلُونَ.

"We went out with the Messenger of Allāh ﷺ to Hunayn while we were new to Islām, just having left disbelief. The disbelievers had a tree which they would spend time with and they would hang their weapons on it (seeking blessings from it). They called this tree Dhāt Anwāt.[5] When we passed by this tree, we said, 'O Messenger of Allāh, make for us something like this to hang our weapons on.' The Messenger of Allāh ﷺ said, 'Allāh is the Greatest! I swear by the One in Whose Hand is my soul, you have said the same as the Children of Israel said to Musa. They said, "O Musa! Make for us a god as they have gods." He said, "Verily, you are a people who are ignorant."'"[6]

They only wanted to seek blessings from the tree. The Prophet ﷺ said they were requesting a god other than Allāh by seeking blessings from a tree. And this is the epitome and essence of *shirk*. When the Messenger of Allāh ﷺ clarified this to them, they returned to the truth and turned to Allāh in repentance. Seeking blessings from graves is a greater sin than what they requested.

---

5. Calling upon the living who are absent and believing that they possess the power to assist, even in their absence, is major *shirk*.

Allāh the Exalted said:

﴿أَمَّن يُجِيبُ الْمُضْطَرَّ إِذَا دَعَاهُ وَيَكْشِفُ السُّوءَ وَيَجْعَلُكُمْ
خُلَفَاءَ الْأَرْضِ ۗ أَإِلَٰهٌ مَّعَ اللَّهِ ۚ قَلِيلًا مَّا تَذَكَّرُونَ﴾

---

[5] Ibn al-Atheer said in *An-Nihāyah*: "This is the name of a specific tree that belonged to the pagans, on which they used to hang their weapons and to which they would go and spend time to seek blessings."

[6] Collected by at-Tirmidhī (2180).

Is not He (better than your gods) Who responds to the distressed one, when he calls Him, and Who removes the evil, and makes you inheritors of the earth, generations after generations. Is there any god with Allāh? Little is that you remember!

[Sūrah an-Naml 27:62]

---

6. Exaggerating the status of the prophets and righteous people to the extent of deifying them is major *shirk* which removes the person from the fold of Islām.

Allāh the Exalted said:

﴿ وَإِذْ قَالَ اللَّهُ يَا عِيسَى ابْنَ مَرْيَمَ أَأَنتَ قُلْتَ لِلنَّاسِ اتَّخِذُونِي وَأُمِّيَ إِلَـٰهَيْنِ مِن دُونِ اللَّهِ ۖ قَالَ سُبْحَانَكَ مَا يَكُونُ لِي أَنْ أَقُولَ مَا لَيْسَ لِي بِحَقٍّ ۚ إِن كُنتُ قُلْتُهُ فَقَدْ عَلِمْتَهُ ۚ تَعْلَمُ مَا فِي نَفْسِي وَلَا أَعْلَمُ مَا فِي نَفْسِكَ ۚ إِنَّكَ أَنتَ عَلَّامُ الْغُيُوبِ ﴾

And (remember) when Allāh will say (on the Day of Resurrection): "O Jesus, son of Maryam! Did you say unto men: 'Worship me and my mother as two gods besides Allāh?'" He will say: "Glory be to You! It was not for me to say what I had no right (to say). Had I said such a thing, You would surely have known it. You know what is in my inner self though I do not know what is in Yours; truly, You, only You, are the All-Knower of all that is hidden and unseen."

[Sūrah al-Mā'idah 5:116]

And Allāh the Exalted said:

﴿ يَا أَهْلَ الْكِتَابِ لَا تَغْلُوا فِي دِينِكُمْ وَلَا تَقُولُوا عَلَى

اللَّهِ إِلَّا الْحَقَّ ۚ إِنَّمَا الْمَسِيحُ عِيسَى ابْنُ مَرْيَمَ رَسُولُ اللَّهِ وَكَلِمَتُهُ أَلْقَاهَا إِلَىٰ مَرْيَمَ وَرُوحٌ مِّنْهُ ۖ فَآمِنُوا بِاللَّهِ وَرُسُلِهِ ۖ وَلَا تَقُولُوا ثَلَاثَةٌ ۚ انتَهُوا خَيْرًا لَّكُمْ ۚ إِنَّمَا اللَّهُ إِلَٰهٌ وَاحِدٌ ۖ سُبْحَانَهُ أَن يَكُونَ لَهُ وَلَدٌ ۘ لَّهُ مَا فِي السَّمَاوَاتِ وَمَا فِي الْأَرْضِ ۗ وَكَفَىٰ بِاللَّهِ وَكِيلًا ﴾

O People of the Scripture (Jews and Christians)! Do not exceed the limits in your religion, nor say of Allāh aught but the truth. The Messiah—Jesus, son of Maryam—was (no more than) a messenger of Allāh and His Word ("Be!" and he was) which He bestowed on Maryam and a spirit created by Him; so believe in Allāh and His messengers. Say not: "Three (trinity)!" Cease! (It is) better for you, for Allāh is (the only) one God, glory be to Him (far Exalted is He) above having a son. To Him belongs all that is in the heavens and all that is in the earth. And Allāh is All-Sufficient as a Disposer of affairs.

[Sūrah an-Nisā' 4:171]

The Prophet Muḥammad ﷺ said:

لاَ تُطْرُونِي كَمَا أَطْرَتِ النَّصَارَى ابْنَ مَرْيَمَ، فَإِنَّمَا أَنَا عَبْدٌ، فَقُولُوا عَبْدُ اللَّهِ وَرَسُولُهُ.

"Do not exaggerate in praising me as the Christians exaggerated in praising the son of Maryam, for I am only a slave. So, call me the slave of Allāh and His Messenger."[7]

[7] *Ṣaḥīḥ al-Bukhārī* 3445

---

7. Fearing the *jinn* or the righteous people (hidden fear), such that the person fears that if he does not do such-and-such, the *jinn* or righteous person will afflict him with evil. This is major *shirk*.

The proof for this is the statement of Allāh ﷻ:

﴿ إِن نَّقُولُ إِلَّا اعْتَرَاكَ بَعْضُ آلِهَتِنَا بِسُوءٍ ۗ قَالَ إِنِّي أُشْهِدُ اللَّهَ وَاشْهَدُوا أَنِّي بَرِيءٌ مِّمَّا تُشْرِكُونَ ﴿٥٤﴾ مِن دُونِهِ ۖ فَكِيدُونِي جَمِيعًا ثُمَّ لَا تُنظِرُونِ ﴿٥٥﴾ ﴾

"All that we say is that some of our gods (false deities) have seized you with evil (madness)." He said, "I call Allāh to witness and bear you witness that I am free from that which you ascribe as partners in worship with Him (Allāh). So plot against me, all of you, and give me no respite."

[Sūrah Hūd 11:54-55]

Fear is from the great aspects of worship performed by the heart which must be sincerely for Allāh. When someone fears something as only Allāh should be feared, they become a pagan. As for natural fear, there is no harm in this. The fear that causes the person to fall short in their obligations or to embark upon the impermissible acts is forbidden, such as the person who avoids enjoining the good and forbidding the evil [due to] fearing the speech of the people or their harms.

---

8. Placing amulets that contain *shirk*, or voodoo, or hanging talismans or charms fearing harm, or to protect against the evil eye or envy, is *shirk*.

Ibn Mas'ūd ﷺ said:

سَمِعْتُ رَسُولَ اللَّهِ صلى الله عليه وسلم يَقُولُ إِنَّ الرُّقَى وَالتَّمَائِمَ وَالتِّوَلَةَ شِرْكٌ.

"I heard the Messenger of Allāh ﷺ saying, 'Verily, spells, amulets, and love potions are *shirk*.'"[8]

And the Prophet ﷺ said:

مَنْ عَلَّقَ تَمِيمَةً فَقَدْ أَشْرَكَ.

"Whoever hangs an amulet has committed *shirk*."[9]

And he said concerning *ruqyah* (incantation) specifically:

لَا بَأْسَ بِالرُّقَى مَا لَمْ يَكُنْ فِيهِ شِرْكٌ.

"There is no harm in incantation that does not contain *shirk* (polytheism)."[10]

The incantations that contain *shirk* are those where help is sought from other than Allāh, and partners are associated with Allāh the Exalted.

Hanging an amulet fearing harm or to protect against the evil eye is minor *shirk*, not major *shirk*, except in the case where help is sought from other than Allāh, or the person speaks with the *jinn* or seeks help from the *jinn*; in this case, it becomes major *shirk*. Thus, it must be specified when this is major *shirk*.

---

9. Going to soothsayers, fortunetellers, and magicians and believing in them is *shirk.*

[8] Collected in *Sunan Abī Dāwūd* (3883).

[9] Collected by Aḥmad (17458)

[10] *Ṣaḥīḥ Muslim* 2200

This is based upon the statement of the Prophet ﷺ:

مَنْ أَتَى عَرَّافًا أَوْ كَاهِنًا، فَصَدَّقَهُ بِمَا يَقُولُ، فَقَدْ كَفَرَ بِمَا أُنْزِلَ عَلَى مُحَمَّدٍ صلى الله عليه وسلم.

"Whoever goes to a fortuneteller or soothsayer and believes what he says, then surely, he has disbelieved in what was revealed to Muḥammad ﷺ."[11]

And in the *ḥadīth* of Ibn Mas'ūd, he said:

مَنْ أَتَى عَرَّافًا، أَوْ سَاحِرًا، أَوْ كَاهِنًا فَسَأَلَهُ فَصَدَّقَهُ بِمَا يَقُولُ، فَقَدْ كَفَرَ بِمَا أُنْزِلَ عَلَى مُحَمَّدٍ صَلَّى اللَّهُ عَلَيْهِ وَسَلَّمَ.

"Whoever goes to a fortuneteller, a magician, or a soothsayer and believes in what he says, then he has surely disbelieved in what was revealed to Muḥammad ﷺ."[12]

Is the disbelief mentioned in these narrations minor disbelief which does not remove the person from the fold of Islām? Or do we refrain from saying whether it removes the person from the fold of Islām or not? The first viewpoint is strong while the second is the viewpoint of Imām Aḥmad.[13]

---

[11] Collected by Aḥmad and al-Hākim.

[12] Collected by Ibn Hibbān from the statements of Ibn Mas'ūd ﷺ.

[13] **Translator's note:** The Permanent Committee of Scholars said: "What is meant by the *ḥadīth:* 'Whoever goes to a soothsayer and believes what he says has disbelieved in that which was revealed to Muḥammad' is that the one who asks a soothsayer a question, believing that he tells the truth and that he knows the unseen, has committed an act of disbelief, because he has gone against the Qur'ān in which Allāh says (interpretation of the meaning): 'Say: "None in the heavens and the earth knows the unseen except Allāh"' (Soorah an-Naml 27:65)." *Fatāwa al-Lajnah ad-Dā'imah lil-Buhooth al-'Ilmiyyah wal-Iftā'* (2/48).

---

10. Hanging a piece of wolf skin on the chest or in the home, believing that it protects against the *jinn*, is *shirk*.

The proof for this was previously mentioned in the 8th affair.

---

11. Sacrificing an animal at the door of the home, fearing the *jinn*, is *shirk*.

The proof for this was previously mentioned in the 3rd and 7th affairs.

---

12. Claiming knowledge of the unseen or claiming to have looked upon the Preserved Tablet is disbelief.

This is based upon the statement of Allāh the Exalted:

﴿ قُل لَّا يَعْلَمُ مَن فِي السَّمَاوَاتِ وَالْأَرْضِ الْغَيْبَ إِلَّا اللَّهُ ﴾

Say: "None in the heavens and the earth knows the unseen except Allāh."

[Sūrah an-Naml 27:65]

And Allāh the Exalted said:

﴿ وَعِندَهُ مَفَاتِحُ الْغَيْبِ لَا يَعْلَمُهَا إِلَّا هُوَ ﴾

And with Him are the keys of all that is hidden; none knows them but He.

[Sūrah al-An'ām 6:59]

Included in this is the claim of some Soofis that the veil of the unseen has been revealed to them.

13. Listening to poems that contain *shirk* and being pleased with it is *shirk*.

That is like the poem *Al-Burda* by al-Būsīrī[14] and similar poems in which the poets exceed the bounds concerning the status of our Prophet Muḥammad ﷺ, and exceed the bounds concerning the status of others, such as the family of the Prophet and the righteous people. And those poems which describe the creation with attributes of the Creator. Some of these poems containing extreme *shirk* are sung during the birthday of the Prophet ﷺ. Thus, it is obligatory to avoid and criticize these poems, in order to protect the Islām of the individuals. May Allāh safeguard the Muslims from *shirk* and its manifestations.

14. Claiming that Allāh becomes incarnate in certain places or in some individuals is major *shirk*.

[14] **Translator's note:** Abū 'Abdillāh Muḥammad bin Sa'īd al-Būsīrī ash-Shadhili (608 AH–696 AH) was a Sanhaji Berber Soofi poet belonging to the Shadhiliyya Soofi order.

2

Mistakes in *'Aqīdah* & *Tawḥīd*: Minor *Shirk*

Secondly: Minor *shirk* (polytheism) and some of its manifestations and means that lead to *shirk*.

---

1. Swearing by other than Allāh without the intent of glorifying this person or thing as one would glorify Allāh; this is minor *shirk*.

The proof for this is the statement of the Prophet ﷺ:

مَنْ حَلَفَ بِغَيْرِ اللَّهِ فَقَدْ كَفَرَ أَوْ أَشْرَكَ.

"Whoever swears an oath by other than Allāh has committed disbelief or polytheism."[1]

And his statement:

مَنْ كَانَ حَالِفًا فَلْيَحْلِفْ بِاللَّهِ أَوْ لِيَصْمُتْ.

---

[1] Collected by Abū Dāwūd (3251).

"Whoever is going to swear an oath, then let them swear by Allāh or remain silent."[2]

But if the person glorifies the creation as only Allāh can be glorified—like those who swear oaths in the name of the graves or righteous people with the intent to glorify them—this is major *shirk*.

If someone swears an oath by other than Allāh without giving it any thought, then this is *shirk* of speech and it is included in the types of minor *shirk*. And the atonement for this statement is to say: "Nothing has the right to be worshiped except Allāh" and then have a strong resolve to never return to swearing oaths by other than Allāh.

---

2. Swearing in the name of honesty[3], a trust, or honor is minor *shirk*.

This is based upon the statement of the Prophet ﷺ:

مَنْ حَلَفَ بِالأَمَانَةِ فَلَيْسَ مِنَّا.

"Whoever swears by honesty is not one of us."[4]

Swearing by any of these affairs is included in the statement of the Prophet ﷺ:

مَنْ حَلَفَ بِغَيْرِ اللَّهِ فَقَدْ كَفَرَ أَوْ أَشْرَكَ.

"Whoever swears an oath by other than Allāh has committed disbelief or polytheism."[5]

Swearing occurs when the person utilizes one of three Arabic letters:

---

[2] Collected by al-Bukhārī (2679).

[3] **Translator's note:** Shaykh Ibn Bāz said, "An example of this is for the person to say: 'I swear by my honesty, I didn't do such-and-such.'"

[4] Collected in *Sunan Abī Dāwūd* (3253).

[5] Collected by Abū Dāwūd (3251).

bā' (الباء), *wāw* (الواو), or *tā'* (التاء). If he uses another letter, such as *fee* (في), it is not swearing.

---

3. Taking graveyards as places for worship is an innovation, evil, impermissible, and a means which leads to worshiping those in the graves.

This is based upon the statement of the Prophet ﷺ:

لَعَنَ اللَّهُ الْيَهُودَ وَالنَّصَارَى، اتَّخَذُوا قُبُورَ أَنْبِيَائِهِمْ مَسْجِدًا.

"Allāh has cursed the Jews and the Christians; they took the graves of their prophets as places of worship."[6]

And his statement:

أَلاَ وَإِنَّ مَنْ كَانَ قَبْلَكُمْ كَانُوا يَتَّخِذُونَ قُبُورَ أَنْبِيَائِهِمْ وَصَالِحِيهِمْ مَسَاجِدَ
أَلاَ فَلاَ تَتَّخِذُوا الْقُبُورَ مَسَاجِدَ إِنِّي أَنْهَاكُمْ عَنْ ذَلِكَ.

"Those who came before you used to take the graves of their prophets and righteous men as places of worship. Do not take graves as places of worship; I forbid you from doing that."[7]

Every place where the people intend to pray becomes a *masjid* (place of worship).

---

4. Praying in the graveyards and supplicating at the graves is an innovation and a means to *shirk*.

This is if the person prays to Allāh alone; but if the person prays to the individual inside the grave in addition to praying to Allāh, this is

[6] *Ṣaḥīḥ al-Bukhārī* 1330

[7] *Ṣaḥīḥ Muslim* 532

absolute, incontestable *shirk*.

There is a prohibition from the Prophet ﷺ against praying in the graveyards. He said:

لاَ تُصَلُّوا إِلَى الْقُبُورِ.

"Don't pray facing towards graves."[8]

'Umar bin al-Khattāb رضي الله عنه saw some people praying towards a grave that they were unaware of, so 'Umar said: "A grave, a grave."

The Prophet ﷺ said:

لاَ تَتَّخِذُوا الْقُبُورَ مَسَاجِدَ.

"Do not take graves as places of worship."[9]

In the *masājid*, Allāh is called upon with the most eloquent, profound supplications; thus, it is known that *du'ā'* is prohibited in the graveyards except if the *du'ā'* is supplicated on behalf of the deceased person in the grave, asking Allāh to have mercy upon them, forgive them, and make them firm. This has come in the Sunnah; those in the graves are in need of the people praying for them.

---

[8] *Ṣaḥīḥ Muslim* 972

[9] *Ṣaḥīḥ Muslim* 532

3

Mistakes Related to Innovations

---

1. Building structures on graves, plastering them, writing on them, and planting trees in the graveyard is an innovation and evil.

The proof for that is the *ḥadīth* of Jābir ﷺ, who said:

نَهَى رَسُولُ اللَّهِ صَلَّى اللَّهُ عَلَيْهِ وَسَلَّمَ أَنْ يُجَصَّصَ الْقَبْرُ وَأَنْ يُقْعَدَ عَلَيْهِ وَأَنْ يُبْنَى عَلَيْهِ.

"The Messenger of Allāh ﷺ forbade plastering over graves, sitting on them, and erecting structures over them."[1]

And in the narration of Thumamah bin Shufa, he said:

كُنَّا مَعَ فَضَالَةَ بْنِ عُبَيْدٍ بِأَرْضِ الرُّومِ فَتُوُفِّيَ صَاحِبٌ لَنَا، فَأَمَرَ فَضَالَةُ بِقَبْرِهِ فَسُوِّيَ، ثُمَّ قَالَ: سَمِعْتُ رَسُولَ اللَّهِ صلى الله عليه وسلم يَأْمُرُ بِتَسْوِيَتِهَا.

"We were with Fadālah bin 'Ubayd in the land of the Romans, and a

---

[1] *Ṣaḥīḥ Muslim* 970

companion of ours died. Fadālah ordered that his grave be made level, then he said: 'I heard the Messenger of Allāh ﷺ commanding that the graves be made level.'"[2]

Abul-Hayāj al-Asadi said:

قَالَ لِي عَلِيُّ بْنُ أَبِي طَالِبٍ أَلَا أَبْعَثُكَ عَلَى مَا بَعَثَنِي عَلَيْهِ رَسُولُ اللَّهِ صَلَّى اللَّهُ عَلَيْهِ وَسَلَّمَ أَنْ لَا تَدَعَ تِمْثَالًا إِلَّا طَمَسْتَهُ وَلَا قَبْرًا مُشْرِفًا إِلَّا سَوَّيْتَهُ.

"'Alī bin Abī Tālib said to me, 'Shall I not send you with the same instructions as the Messenger of Allāh ﷺ sent me? Do not leave any image without defacing it or any built-up grave without leveling it.'"[3]

And in another narration, he said: "Any picture without defacing it."

---

2. Celebrating various birthdays with the intention of coming closer to Allāh with that.

An example of this is the celebration of the birthday of the Prophet ﷺ, or celebrating the migration, the new year, or the Night of Ascension. These celebrations are innovations because the intent is to draw close to Allāh with these actions, and no one can come close to Allāh except by performing the actions He has legislated, and Allāh is not worshiped except by what He legislated. Thus, every newly invented matter in the religion is an innovation, and innovation is prohibited.

Allāh the Exalted said:

﴿ أَمْ لَهُمْ شُرَكَاءُ شَرَعُوا لَهُم مِّنَ الدِّينِ مَا لَمْ يَأْذَن بِهِ اللَّهُ ﴾

---

[2] *Sunan an-Nasā'ī* 2030

[3] *Ṣaḥīḥ Muslim* 969

Or have they partners with Allāh, who have instituted for them a religion which Allāh has not allowed?

[Sūrah ash-Shūrā 42:21]

The Prophet ﷺ said:

مَنْ أَحْدَثَ فِي أَمْرِنَا هَذَا مَا لَيْسَ مِنْهُ فَهُوَ رَدٌّ.

"Whoever introduces something into this affair of ours which is not from it, it is rejected."[4]

And he said:

مَنْ عَمِلَ عَمَلاً لَيْسَ عَلَيْهِ أَمْرُنَا فَهُوَ رَدٌّ.

"Whoever does an action which is not from our affair, it is rejected."[5]

The Prophet ﷺ said:

وَكُلَّ مُحْدَثَةٍ بِدْعَةٌ وَكُلَّ بِدْعَةٍ ضَلاَلَةٌ.

"And every newly invented matter is an innovation and every innovation is misguidance."[6]

The Messenger of Allāh ﷺ said:

عَلَيْكُمْ بِسُنَّتِي وَسُنَّةِ الْخُلَفَاءِ الْمَهْدِيِّينَ الرَّاشِدِينَ تَمَسَّكُوا بِهَا وَعَضُّوا عَلَيْهَا بِالنَّوَاجِذِ وَإِيَّاكُمْ وَمُحْدَثَاتِ الْأُمُورِ فَإِنَّ كُلَّ مُحْدَثَةٍ بِدْعَةٌ وَكُلَّ بِدْعَةٍ ضَلاَلَةٌ.

"It is upon you to adhere to my way (Sunnah) and the way of the rightly guided successors who come after me. Adhere to it and bite onto it with your molar teeth (i.e., cling firmly to it). Beware of newly

---

[4] *Ṣaḥīḥ Muslim* 1718

[5] *Ṣaḥīḥ Muslim* 1718

[6] *Sunan an-Nasā'ī* 1578

invented matters, for every newly invented matter is an innovation and every innovation is a going-astray."[7]

And there are other narrations proving the prohibition of innovating in the religion of Allāh, and prohibiting the people from enacting legislation for themselves in worship and actions to draw near to Allāh, which He nor His Messenger ﷺ did not legislate.

---

3. Celebrating the various innovated celebrations like the Prophet's birthday, New Year's Day, or Mother's Day.

This is prohibited from three angles:

1) It is an innovation which has not been legislated. It has only been legislated by the desires of the people. These celebrations, and enjoying and rejoicing from these acts, is not permissible. They cannot be established and the people cannot be pleased with it.

2) The Muslims have two Eids and no more: Eid al-Fitr ,when the people are happy due to the completion of the fast, and Eid al-Adha, which is the day of sacrifice and the following days. The Prophet ﷺ said:

يَوْمُ عَرَفَةَ، وَيَوْمُ النَّحْرِ، وَأَيَّامُ التَّشْرِيقِ عِيدُنَا أَهْلَ الْإِسْلَامِ.

"The Day of 'Arafah, the Day of Sacrifice (an-Nahr), and the Days of Tashreeq are our Eid, for the people of Islām."[8]

And the Prophet ﷺ said:

إِنَّ لِكُلِّ قَوْمٍ عِيدًا وَهَذَا عِيدُنَا.

---

[7] Narrated by at-Tirmidhī (2676), Abū Dāwūd (4607), and Ibn Mājah (42). This *ḥadīth* was classed as *ṣaḥīḥ* by al-Albāni in *Ṣaḥīḥ al-Jāmi'* (2549), from the *ḥadīth* of al-'Irbād bin Sāriyah.

[8] Narrated by an-Nasā'ī (3004), at-Tirmidhī (773), and Abū Dāwūd (2419), from the *ḥadīth* of 'Uqbah bin 'Āmir. Classed as *ṣaḥīḥ* by al-Albāni in *Ṣaḥīḥ Abī Dāwūd*.

> "Every people has its festival (Eid), and this is our festival."[9]

The phrase "our" means the Muslims. This shows that the festival is connected to the religions.

3) Celebrating these festivals is imitation of the disbelievers—from the People of the Book and other than them—in the holidays they innovated which were not legislated. There is no doubt that we have been commanded to not imitate them and to cut off the matters resembling them.

---

4. Celebrating the middle of the month of Sha'bān.

Specifying this night with worship has no proof, so it is an innovation. The narrations mentioning specifying this night are not authentic according to the scholars. Specifying this night is among the innovations prohibited by the evidence.

---

5. Specifying the month of Rajab for fasting.

This is an innovation. The narrations that mention the virtue of the month of Rajab are not authentic; rather, they are all extremely weak narrations, so they cannot be relied upon.

---

6. Specifying certain days, weeks, or months for worship is not legislated.

This specification is an innovation. Specifying particular seasons for worship can only come by way of the legislation of Islām. Thus, whatever has proof from the legislation of Islām, then we work according to it. As for specifying a particular time for worship without proof from the legislation of Islām, this is from the newly

[9] *Ṣaḥīḥ al-Bukhārī* 3931

invented matters.

---

7. Performing any act of worship that has no basis in the legislation in order to draw close to Allāh, is an innovation.

All of this is innovation, and innovation is blameworthy in the legislation due to the statement of the Prophet ﷺ:

وَكُلَّ بِدْعَةٍ ضَلَالَةٌ.

"And every innovation is misguidance."[10]

This is general to include every newly invented matter used to draw close to Allāh; it is all misguidance. There is no innovation in the religion known as "good innovation"; rather, all innovation is repugnant. It is not permissible to innovate in the religion nor is it permissible to practice innovation. Each and every good can be found in the worship of the Companions of the Messenger of Allāh ﷺ, which they inherited from the guidance of the Prophet ﷺ. Ibn Mas'ūd رضي الله عنه said:

كُلُّ عِبَادَةٍ لَمْ يَتَعَبَّدْهَا أَصْحَابُ رَسُولِ اللَّهِ صَلَّى اللَّهُ عَلَيْهِ وَسَلَّمَ، فَلَا تَعَبَّدُوهَا فَإِنَّ الْأَوَّلَ لَمْ يَدَعْ لِلْآخِرِ مَقَالًا.

"Every act of worship with which the Companions of the Messenger of Allāh ﷺ did not worship, then don't worship with it, because surely the first generation did not leave the later generations any room to speak."[11]

And how wonderful is the statement of the one who said:

وَكُلُ خَيْرٍ فِي اتِّبَاعِ مَنْ سَلَفْ وَكُلُّ شَرٍّ فِي ابْتِدَاعِ مَنْ خَلَفْ.

---

[10] *Sunan an-Nasā'ī* 1578

[11] **Translator's note:** Collected by Imām ash-Shātibi in his book *Al-Itisam*.

"Every good can be found in those who preceded, while every evil can be found in those who came later."

4

Mistakes Related to Purification

1. Pronouncing the intention at the start of *wudoo'*.

This is not permissible, because the place of the intention is the heart. Our Prophet—who is our leader—did not pronounce his intention. The legislated manner in which the intention is made,is for the heart of the person performing *wudoo'* to intend that his *wudoo'* is for the prayer or for touching the *mus'haf* or the like. This is the intention. He intends this act of worship with his heart. The Prophet ﷺ incited the *ummah* to begin the worship of *wudoo'* with saying: "In the name of Allāh," and nothing else. Thus, starting the *wudoo'* by pronouncing the intention is in opposition to what he directed us to and commanded us with.

2. Lack of concern for the prescribed *wudoo'* and *ghusl*, and apathy in regard to learning the rulings of purification.

Apathy in regard to the *wudoo'* and *ghusl*[1] must be avoided by the

[1] **Translator's note:** *Ghusl* is the shower taken when the person is in a state of major impurity, such as the impurity following sexual discharge, menses, or postpartum bleeding.

Muslims, because purification, *wudoo'*, and *ghusl* are conditions for the correctness of the prayer. Thus, the person who has no concern for these matters, then his prayer will not be correct due to his negligence of an obligatory condition.

The Prophet ﷺ said to Laqit bin Sabirah:

أسبغ الْوُضُوءِ.

"Perfect the *wudoo'*.[2]

The Prophet ﷺ said:

وَيْلٌ لِلْأَعْقَابِ مِنْ النَّارِ!

"Woe to the heels from the Hellfire!"[3]

This is because the heels are a place which may be forgotten while performing the *wudoo'*, and the other parts of the body carry a similar ruling. Therefore, it is obligatory to perfect and complete the *wudoo'* over all the limbs. This is by placing water over all of them except for the head. It is sufficient to wipe most of the head along with the ears. The ears are part of the head, as the Prophet ﷺ said:

الأُذُنَانِ مِنَ الرَّأْسِ.

"The two ears are part of the head."[4]

Consequently, it is necessary for the Muslim to study the rules and regulations of *wudoo'*. It is recommended for the perfection of the *wudoo'* that he wash each part three times following the example of the Prophet ﷺ, and in order to obtain the virtue of the prayer. The Prophet ﷺ said:

---

[2] Collected by Abū Dāwūd and at-Tirmidhī.

[3] Narrated by al-Bukhārī (96) and Muslim (241).

[4] Collected in *Sunan Ibn Mājah.*

مَنْ أَتَمَّ الْوُضُوءَ كَمَا أَمَرَهُ اللَّهُ تَعَالَى، فَالصَّلَوَاتُ الْمَكْتُوبَاتُ، كَفَّارَاتٌ لِمَا بَيْنَهُنَّ.

"Whoever completes the *wudoo'* as Allāh the Exalted has commanded him, then his obligatory prayers will be expiation for the interval between them."[5]

The narrations concerning the virtue of perfecting the *wudoo'* and its expiation from sins are numerous.

---

3. Whispers during *wudoo'* which cause the person to wash his limbs more than three times and doubt his *wudoo'*.

This whisper is from the Shaytān, and the Prophet ﷺ did not wash his limbs more than three times during *wudoo'*. It has been narrated concerning the Prophet ﷺ that he would:

توضأ ثلاثا ثلاثا.

"Wash each limb in *wudoo'* three times."[6]

It is obligatory upon the Muslim to repel these whispers and doubts after the completion of the *wudoo'*, and he should not wash his limbs more than three times. This will repel the whispers which are from the plot of the Shaytān.

---

4. Wasting water.

This is prohibited due to the general meaning of the statement of Allāh the Exalted:

﴿ وَلَا تُسْرِفُوا ۚ إِنَّهُ لَا يُحِبُّ الْمُسْرِفِينَ ﴾

[5] *Ṣaḥīḥ Muslim* 231

[6] Collected in *Ṣaḥīḥ al-Bukhārī*.

But waste not by extravagance; certainly He (Allāh) likes not those who waste by extravagance.

[Sūrah al-A'rāf 7:31]

This is likewise prohibited due to the narration of the Prophet ﷺ:

أَنَّ النَّبِيَّ صَلَّى اللَّهُ عَلَيْهِ وَسَلَّمَ مَرَّ بِسَعْدٍ وَهُوَ يَتَوَضَّأُ فَقَالَ: مَا هَذَا السَّرَفُ يَا سَعْدُ؟ قَالَ: أَفِي الْوُضُوءِ سَرَفٌ؟ قَالَ: نَعَمْ، وَإِنْ كُنْتَ عَلَى نَهْرٍ جَارٍ.

"The Prophet ﷺ passed by Sa'd when he was performing *wudoo'*, and he said, 'What is this extravagance, O Sa'd?' He said, 'Can there be any extravagance in *wudoo'*?' He said, 'Yes, even if you are on the bank of a flowing river.'"[7]

---

5. Mentioning Allāh in the toilet areas or bringing something into the toilet area with the remembrance of Allāh on it.

This is hated, and the Muslim must avoid this. It has been narrated by Ibn 'Umar ﷺ:

أَنَّ رَجُلاً، مَرَّ وَرَسُولُ اللَّهِ صلى الله عليه وسلم يَبُولُ فَسَلَّمَ فَلَمْ يَرُدَّ عَلَيْهِ.

"A man passed by while the Messenger of Allāh ﷺ was urinating. [The man] greeted him with *salām*, but he did not return the greeting."[8]

This is because returning the *salām* is from remembrance of Allāh.

---

6. Wiping the head more than one time.

This is in opposition to the guidance of the Prophet ﷺ, because he would only wipe his head one time. It has been narrated by 'Alī ﷺ in his description of the *wudoo'* of the Prophet ﷺ that he said:

[7] Collected by Imām Aḥmad (6768) and Ibn Mājah (419).

[8] *Ṣaḥīḥ Muslim* 370

وَمَسَحَ بِرَأْسِهِ وَاحِدَةً.

"He wiped his head once."[9]

Abū Dāwūd said: "All the authentic *ahādeeth* narrated by 'Uthmān indicate that the head is to be wiped once."

---

7. Wiping the neck.

This is a mistake; in fact, some scholars consider this to be an innovation because nothing like this has been affirmed from the Prophet ﷺ. The narrations mentioning this are fabrications. Some scholars have mentioned wiping the neck, but they were not aware that these narrations are not authentic. Thus, it is not prescribed to wipe the neck. It is necessary to avoid this in order to protect the legislation of Islām from additions.

---

8. Wiping the bottom of the *khuff*[10] or sock when wiping over the socks.

This is a mistake and ignorance because the Prophet ﷺ wiped over the top of the *khuff*. Mugheerah bin Shuba said:

رأيت رسول الله صلى الله عليه وسلم يمسح على ظهور الخفين.

"I saw the Messenger of Allāh ﷺ wiping over the top of the *khuff*."[11]

'Alī bin Abī Tālib رضي الله عنه said:

لَوْ كَانَ اَلدِّينُ بِالرَّأْيِ لَكَانَ أَسْفَلُ اَلْخُفِّ أَوْلَى بِالْمَسْحِ مِنْ أَعْلَاهُ، وَقَدْ

---

[9] Collected by Abū Dāwūd, an-Nasā'ī, and at-Tirmidhī, and collected in *Buloogh al-Marām* (34).

[10] Leather socks.

[11] Collected by Abū Dāwūd, at-Tirmidhī, and Aḥmad.

رَأَيْتُ رَسُولَ اَللَّهِ (صلى الله عليه وسلم) يَمْسَحُ عَلَى ظَاهِرِ خُفَّيْهِ.

"If the religion was based upon opinion, it would have been more befitting to wipe the bottom of the *khuff* and not the top. But I saw the Messenger of Allāh ﷺ wiping over the top of the *khuff*."[12]

---

9. Performing *istinjā'*[13] (الاستنجاء) after passing wind.

Passing wind does not require *istinjā'* (cleaning the private area with water). *Istinjā'* is only performed after urinating or defecating, so it is not necessary to perform *istinjā'* after passing wind, before performing *wudoo'*, as some of the people do. The legislative text does not indicate that one should do such; rather, the texts show that the person only has to perform *wudoo'* after passing wind. And all praises belong to Allāh for His ease.

Imām Aḥmad said: "There is no mention in the Book of Allāh or the Sunnah of His Messenger that passing wind requires the person to perform *istinjā'*; the only thing upon him is to perform *wudoo'*."

---

[12] *Buloogh al-Marām* 60

[13] **Translator's note:** *Istinjā'* means removing with water whatever has been passed from the front or back passages of urine or feces.

5

Mistakes Regarding the Prayer

---

1. Abandoning the prayer completely.

This is disbelief, may Allāh save us and our brother from that. The Qur'ān, Sunnah, and consensus of the *ummah* prove that the complete abandonment of the prayer is disbelief. Allāh the Exalted said:

﴿ فَإِن تَابُوا وَأَقَامُوا الصَّلَاةَ وَآتَوُا الزَّكَاةَ فَإِخْوَانُكُمْ فِي الدِّينِ ﴾

But if they repent, establish the prayer, and give *zakāh*, then they are your brethren in religion.

[Sūrah at-Tawbah 9:11]

﴿ مَا سَلَكَكُمْ فِي سَقَرَ ﴿٤٢﴾ قَالُوا لَمْ نَكُ مِنَ الْمُصَلِّينَ ﴿٤٣﴾ ﴾

"What caused you to enter the blazing Fire?" They said, "We were not of those who prayed."

[Sūrah al-Muddaththir 74:42-43]

The proof from the Sunnah is the *ḥadīth* of Jābir رضي الله عنه. The Prophet ﷺ

said:

إِنَّ بَيْنَ الرَّجُلِ وَبَيْنَ الشِّرْكِ وَالْكُفْرِ تَرْكَ الصَّلاةِ.

"Verily, between the person and polytheism and disbelief is the abandonment of the prayer."[1]

The Prophet ﷺ said:

الْعَهْدُ الَّذِي بَيْنَنَا وَبَيْنَهُمُ الصَّلاةُ فَمَنْ تَرَكَهَا فَقَدْ كَفَرَ.

"The covenant that distinguishes between us and them is the prayer; thus, whoever abandons it has disbelieved."[2]

As for the consensus, 'Abdullāh bin Shaqiq ﷺ said:

كَانَ أَصْحَابُ مُحَمَّدٍ صلى الله عليه وسلم لاَ يَرَوْنَ شَيْئًا مِنَ الأَعْمَالِ تَرْكُهُ كُفْرٌ غَيْرَ الصَّلاَةِ.

"The Companions of the Prophet ﷺ did not think that abandoning any deed was disbelief, apart from neglecting the prayer."[3]

---

2. Delaying the prayer past its time.

﴿ إِنَّ الصَّلَاةَ كَانَتْ عَلَى الْمُؤْمِنِينَ كِتَابًا مَّوْقُوتًا ﴾

Verily, the prayer is enjoined on the believers at fixed hours.

[Sūrah an-Nisā' 4:103]

This means that the prayers are set at certain times, so to delay them past the obligatory time is a major sin. And help is sought with Allāh. Anas ﷺ said that the Prophet ﷺ said:

---

[1] *Ṣaḥīḥ Muslim* 82

[2] Narrated by Buraydah bin al-Husayb ﷺ, *Sunan Ibn Mājah.*

[3] *Jāmi' at-Tirmidhī* 2622

تِلْكَ صَلَاةُ الْمُنَافِقِ يَجْلِسُ يَرْقُبُ الشَّمْسَ حَتَّى إِذَا كَانَتْ بَيْنَ قَرْنَيْ الشَّيْطَانِ قَامَ فَنَقَرَ أَرْبَعًا لَا يَذْكُرُ اللَّهَ فِيهَا إِلَّا قَلِيلًا.

"That is the prayer of the hypocrite. He sits watching the sun until it is between the horns of the Shaytān (just before sunset), then he stands and pecks four times, and he does not remember Allāh except a little."[4]

If this is the prayer of the hypocrite, then how about the person who delays the prayer until the time completely goes out, without any excuse? More than one scholar has given the verdict that the person who abandons the obligatory prayer until the time expires, without a resolve to perform this prayer, has disbelieved.

---

3. Neglecting prayer in congregation, constantly or sometimes, for the men who are able to pray in congregation.

Establishing the prayer in congregation in the *masjid* is obligatory except for the person with a legislative excuse—in that case, it is allowable for him to remain behind. The Messenger of Allāh ﷺ said:

مَنْ سَمِعَ النِّدَاءَ فَلَمْ يَأْتِهِ فَلَا صَلَاةَ لَهُ إِلا مِنْ عُذْرٍ.

"Whoever hears the call to prayer and does not respond, there is no prayer for him, except for the one who has an excuse."[5]

Allāh the Exalted said:

﴿ وَارْكَعُوا مَعَ الرَّاكِعِينَ ﴾

Bow with those who bow.

[Sūrah al-Baqarah 2:43]

[4] *Ṣaḥīḥ Muslim* 195

[5] *Sunan Ibn Mājah* 793

The Prophet ﷺ said:

وَالَّذِي نَفْسِي بِيَدِهِ لَقَدْ هَمَمْتُ أَنْ آمُرَ بِحَطَبٍ فَيُحْطَبَ ثُمَّ آمُرَ بِالصَّلَاةِ فَيُؤَذَّنَ لَهَا ثُمَّ آمُرَ رَجُلًا فَيَؤُمَّ النَّاسَ ثُمَّ أُخَالِفَ إِلَى رِجَالٍ فَأُحَرِّقَ عَلَيْهِمْ بُيُوتَهُمْ.

"By the One in Whose Hand is my soul, I had thought of ordering wood to be gathered, then I would command the call to prayer to be given, and I would appoint a man to lead the people in prayer, then I would go to men [who do not attend the congregational prayer] and burn their houses down around them."[6]

---

4. The absence of ease and tranquility throughout the prayer.

This is from ignorance which has become commonplace and widespread, and it is plain sin, because tranquility is a pillar of the prayer and the prayer is not correct without it. The *ḥadīth* of the man who prayed badly is clear proof of this. The meaning of ease and tranquility in the prayer during the various movements—such as bowing, standing from bowing, prostrating, and sitting between the two prostrations—is that the person does not move until his bones settle in that position, and he does not rush to move to another pillar of the prayer until each vertebra has settled in its position. The Prophet ﷺ said to the man who rushed his prayer and did not pray with tranquility:

ارْجِعْ فَصَلِّ، فَإِنَّكَ لَمْ تُصَلِّ.بُيُوتَهُمْ.

"Go back and pray, for indeed you have not prayed."[7]

In the narration of Rifa'ah bin Rāfi', the Prophet ﷺ said to the man who prayed badly:

---

[6] *Ṣaḥīḥ al-Bukhārī* 7224; *Ṣaḥīḥ Muslim* 651

[7] *Ṣaḥīḥ al-Bukhārī* 6667

وَيَضَعُ كَفَّيْهِ عَلَى رُكْبَتَيْهِ حَتَّى تَطْمَئِنَّ مَفَاصِلُهُ وَيَسْتَوِي
اللَّهُ لِمَنْ حَمِدَهُ، وَيَسْتَوِي قَائِمًا حَتَّى يَأْخُذَ كُلُّ عَظْمٍ

ماحـ

"Then pronounce the *takbeer* (saying 'Allāh is the Greatest'), then bow and place your palms on your knees until your joints are at ease and even. Then say: 'Allāh responds to those who praise Him,' and stand up straight until each bone takes its position."[8]

---

5. The absence of focus and devoutness in the prayer, and a lot of movement in the prayer.

Focus and solemnity (*khushoo'*) is in the heart, the stillness of the limbs, and humility towards Allāh. Allāh praised His slaves in His statement:

﴿ الَّذِينَ هُمْ فِي صَلَاتِهِمْ خَاشِعُونَ ﴾

Those who offer their prayers with all solemnity and full submissiveness.

[Sūrah al-Mu'minūn 23:2]

And His statement:

﴿ إِنَّهُمْ كَانُوا يُسَارِعُونَ فِي الْخَيْرَاتِ وَيَدْعُونَنَا رَغَبًا وَرَهَبًا ۖ وَكَانُوا لَنَا خَاشِعِينَ ﴾

Verily, they used to hasten to do good deeds, and they used to call on Us with hope and fear, and used to humble themselves before Us.

[Sūrah al-Anbiyā' 21:90]

It is necessary for the slave to keep their limbs still and their heart

[8] *Ṣaḥīḥ al-Bukhārī* 757; *Ṣaḥīḥ Muslim* 397

solemn and focused in order to perfect the reward for their prayer. It has been narrated from 'Ammār bin Yāsir ﷺ that he said: "I heard the Prophet ﷺ say:

إِنَّ الرَّجُلَ لَيَنْصَرِفُ وَمَا كُتِبَ لَهُ، إِلَّا عُشْرُ صَلَاتِهِ تُسْعُهَا ثُمْنُهَا سُبْعُهَا
سُدْسُهَا خُمْسُهَا رُبْعُهَا ثُلُثُهَا نِصْفُهَا.

"'A man returns after praying and it has only been written for him, a tenth of his prayer, or a ninth, or an eighth, or a seventh, or a sixth, or a fifth, or a third, or half.'"[9]

The reason for his reward being decreased is due to the deficiency of focus and solemnity (*khushoo'*) in his heart, his hands, and the like.

---

6. Purposely preceding the *imām* in the prayer.

This invalidates the prayer or the *rak'ah*. Whoever bows before the *imām*, his *rak'ah* is invalid. His *rak'ah* is only valid if he bows after the *imām*. This applies to the other pillars of the prayer as well. It is obligatory upon the person to follow the *imām* and not precede him. He does not precede the *imām* or lag behind him by a pillar or more. The Prophet ﷺ said:

إِنَّمَا جُعِلَ الإِمَامُ لِيُؤْتَمَّ بِهِ فَإِذَا كَبَّرَ فَكَبِّرُوا وَلاَ تُكَبِّرُوا حَتَّى يُكَبِّرَ وَإِذَا رَكَعَ
فَارْكَعُوا وَلاَ تَرْكَعُوا حَتَّى يَرْكَعَ.

"The *imām* is appointed only to be followed; when he says, 'Allāh is the Greatest,' say, 'Allāh is the Greatest,' and do not say 'Allāh is the Greatest' until he says 'Allāh is the Greatest.' When he bows, bow; and do not bow until he bows."[10]

As for the one who forgets or is ignorant, he is excused.

---

[9] *Sunan Abī Dāwūd* 796

[10] *Sunan Abī Dāwūd* 603

7. Standing to complete the missed *rak'ah* before the *imām* says the second *tasleem.*[11]

This is based upon what has been collected in *Ṣaḥīḥ Muslim*. The Messenger of Allāh ﷺ said:

لَا تَسْبِقُونِي بِالرُّكُوعِ، وَلَا بِالسُّجُودِ، وَلَا بِالْقِيَامِ، وَلَا بِالِانْصِرَافِ.

"Do not precede me in bowing, prostrating, standing, or departing."[12]

The scholars said: The meaning of "departing" is the *tasleem* at the end of the prayer. It is called "departing" because it allows the person to depart afterwards, and he only departs after the second *tasleem*. The person who has to make up part of his prayer waits until the *imām* has completed his prayer, then he stands and completes what he has missed from his prayer. And Allāh knows best.

8. Pronouncing the intention at the time of prayer.

This is an innovation, and I have previously mentioned the evidence for the prohibition of innovation. The Prophet ﷺ never audibly pronounced his intention for the prayer. Ibn al-Qayyim رحمه الله said: "When the Prophet ﷺ stood for the prayer, he said, 'Allāh is the Greatest.' And he did not say anything before it. He absolutely did not utter his intention. He did not say, 'I will pray for Allāh prayer such-and-such, facing the direction of prayer, with four units of prayer, leading those behind me, or being led.' He did not say, 'I am

---

11 **Translator's note:** Shaykh 'Uthaymeen رحمه الله said: "It is prescribed that the person should not stand until the *imām* has said *salām* the second time, because the prayer concludes with the second *tasleem*. Some of the scholars say that if the person praying behind the *imām* stands before the second *tasleem*, his prayer becomes an optional prayer; meaning, this prayer does not count as his obligatory prayer. Thus, it is obligatory upon those praying behind the *imām* to wait until the *imām* says the second *tasleem* before standing." (*Fatāwā Noor 'Alad-Darb*, tape #290)

12 *Ṣaḥīḥ Muslim* 426

performing a prayer during its time or making up a prayer.' All of this is an innovation. There is not a single narration with an authentic chain of narration or a weak chain of narration, or a fabricated *ḥadīth,* which mentions him doing any of this. This was not done by the Companions, those who followed the Companions, or the four Imāms."[13]

---

9. Not reciting Soorah al-Fātiḥah in the prayer.

The recitation of al-Fātihah[14] is a pillar of the prayer and the prayer is not correct for the person who does not recite al-Fātihah. The Prophet ﷺ said:

مَنْ صَلَّى صَلاَةً لَمْ يَقْرَأْ فِيهَا بِفَاتِحَةِ الْكِتَابِ فَهِيَ خِدَاجٌ فَهِيَ خِدَاجٌ فَهِيَ خِدَاجٌ غَيْرُ تَمَامٍ ''، قَالَهَا ثَلاَثًا.

"Whoever offers a prayer and does not recite the opening chapter of the Book, then it is defective, incomplete." (He said this three times).[15]

The Prophet ﷺ said:

لاَ صَلاَةَ لِمَنْ لَمْ يَقْرَأْ بِفَاتِحَةِ الْكِتَابِ.

"There is no prayer for the one who does not recite the opening of the Book."[16]

And the Prophet ﷺ said:

لعلكم تقرؤون خلف إمامكم، قلنا: نعم. قال: لا تفعلوا إلا بفاتحة الكتاب، فإنه لا صلاة لمن لم يقرأ بها.

---

[13] *Zād al-Ma'ād* or *Prophetic Guidance*

[14] **Translator's note:** Al-Fātihah is the opening chapter of the Qur'ān.

[15] *Ṣaḥīḥ Muslim* 395

[16] *Ṣaḥīḥ al-Bukhārī* 756

"Perhaps you recite behind your *imām*?" They said, "Yes," He said, "Do not do that, except for the opening of the Book (al-Fātihah), for there is no prayer for the one who does not recite it."[17]

The recitation of al-Fatihah for those praying behind the *imām* is always done in silent prayer. As for the prayers in which the recitation is aloud, there is a known difference of opinion concerning this matter. The majority of the scholars say the recitation is waived in this case, but to recite it is to free oneself of blame and safer for the religion. Most of the scholars who say that it is waived in this case still say that reciting it is recommended.

---

10. Reciting the Qur'ān in *rukoo'* and *sujood.*

This is prohibited due to the *ḥadīth* of Ibn 'Abbās ﵄. The Prophet ﷺ said:

أَلَا إِنِّي نُهِيتُ أَنْ أَقْرَأَ رَاكِعًا أَوْ سَاجِدًا.

"Verily, I have been forbidden from reciting the Qur'ān when bowing or prostrating."[18]

'Alī bin Abī Tālib ﵁ said:

نَهَانِي رَسُولُ اللَّهِ صَلَّى اللَّهُ عَلَيْهِ وَسَلَّمَ أَنْ أَقْرَأَ رَاكِعًا أَوْ سَاجِدًا.

"The Messenger of Allāh ﷺ forbade me from reciting Qur'ān while bowing and prostrating."[19]

---

11. Raising the eyes towards the sky during the prayer or looking to the right and left without a need.

---

[17] *Sunan Abī Dāwūd* 823

[18] *Sunan an-Nasā'ī* 1045

[19] *Ṣaḥīḥ Muslim* 479

Raising the eyes towards the sky during the prayer is prohibited and there is a threat for those who do so. The Messenger of Allāh ﷺ said:

لَيَنْتَهِيَنَّ أَقْوَامٌ يَرْفَعُونَ أَبْصَارَهُمْ إِلَى السَّمَاءِ فِي الصَّلاَةِ أَوْ لاَ تَرْجِعُ إِلَيْهِمْ.

"The people will either stop lifting their eyes to the sky during the prayer or their eyesight will not return to them."[20]

As for looking around during the prayer, this decreases the prayer of the slave if the person does not look completely in another direction; but if he looks completely in another direction, it invalidates the prayer. It has been narrated from Ā'ishah رضي الله عنها that she said:

سَأَلْتُ رَسُولَ اللَّهِ صلى الله عليه وسلم عَنْ الاِلْتِفَاتِ فِي الصَّلاَةِ فَقَالَ هُوَ اخْتِلاَسٌ يَخْتَلِسُهُ الشَّيْطَانُ مِنْ صَلاَةِ الْعَبْدِ.

"I asked the Messenger of Allāh ﷺ about looking around in the prayer. He replied, 'It is a way of stealing by which the Shaytān takes away (a portion) from the prayer of a person.'"[21]

And the Prophet ﷺ said:

إِيَّاكَ وَالاِلْتِفَاتَ فِي الصَّلاَةِ فَإِنَّ الاِلْتِفَاتَ فِي الصَّلاَةِ هَلَكَةٌ.

"Beware of looking around in the prayer, for surely looking around during the prayer is destruction."[22]

And there are other narrations prohibiting looking around during the prayer.

---

12. Squatting during the prayer, and spreading the arms in prostration.

[20] *Ṣaḥīḥ Muslim* 428

[21] *Ṣaḥīḥ al-Bukhārī* 751

[22] *Jāmi' at-Tirmidhī* 589

Squatting is prohibited based on the *ḥadīth* narrated by Abū Hurayrah ﷺ. He said:

نَهَانِي رَسُولُ اللَّهِ صَلَّى اللَّهُ عَلَيْهِ وَسَلَّمَ عَنْ ثَلَاثَةٍ عَنْ نَقْرَةٍ كَنَقْرَةِ الدِّيكِ وَإِقْعَاءٍ كَإِقْعَاءِ الْكَلْبِ وَالْتِفَاتٍ كَالْتِفَاتِ الثَّعْلَبِ.

"The Messenger of Allāh ﷺ prohibited me from three things: from pecking like a rooster pecks, squatting like a dog squats, and looking around like a fox looks around."[23]

The Messenger of Allāh ﷺ forbade the people from spreading their arms like a beast of prey does. The Prophet ﷺ said:

إِذَا سَجَدَ أَحَدُكُمْ فَلْيَعْتَدِلْ وَلَا يَفْتَرِشْ ذِرَاعَيْهِ افْتِرَاشَ الْكَلْبِ.

"When one of you prostrates, let him be balanced and not spread his arms [like] the spreading of a dog."[24]

---

13. Wearing transparent or flimsy clothes that do not hide the *'awrah*.[25]

This invalidates the prayer because covering the *'awrah* is a condition for the correctness of the prayer. The *'awrah* of the man, according to the correct viewpoint, is between the navel and the knee. Likewise, it is obligatory to cover the two shoulders or one of them. This is based upon the statement of Allāh the Exalted:

---

[23] Collected by Aḥmad.

[24] *Sunan Ibn Mājah* 941

[25] **Translator's note:** The *'awrah* of a man is the area between the navel and the knee. Shaykh Ibn 'Uthaymeen رحمه الله said, "There are several opinions concerning the matter: One is that the knee is included in the *'awrah* so it must be covered. The second opinion is that the navel and the knee are both part of the *'awrah* so they must both be covered. The third opinion—which is the well-known view among our *madh'hab*—is that the navel and the knee are not included in the *'awrah*, so they do not have to be covered. This is based on the definition of the *'awrah* as being 'between the navel and the knee.'" (*Ash-Sharh al-Mumti'* 2/160)

﴿ يَا بَنِي آدَمَ خُذُوا زِينَتَكُمْ عِندَ كُلِّ مَسْجِدٍ ﴾

O Children of Ādam! Take your adornment while praying.

[Sūrah al-A'rāf 7:31]

One garment is sufficient to cover the *'awrah,* based upon the *ḥadīth* of 'Umar bin Abī Salamah ﵁.:

أَنَّهُ رَأَى رَسُولَ اللَّهِ صلى الله عليه وسلم يُصَلِّي فِي ثَوْبٍ وَاحِدٍ مُشْتَمِلاً بِهِ فِي بَيْتِ أُمِّ سَلَمَةَ وَاضِعًا طَرَفَيْهِ عَلَى عَاتِقَيْهِ.

"He saw the Messenger of Allāh ﷺ praying in one garment in the house of Umm Salamah. He was completely covered by it and had put both ends over his shoulders."[26]

Imām Ibn Qudāmah said: "It is required is to wear something that conceals the color of the skin. If it is light and shows the color of the skin underneath it, and one can tell whether the skin is white or red, then it is not permissible to pray in it, because it does not cover properly." (*Al-Mughni* 1/337).

---

14. Women not wearing a head covering or not covering their feet during the prayer.

The *'awrah* for the woman during the prayer is her entire body except for the face, and there is no harm in her covering her face during the prayer if a need arises, such as men passing by. Thus, it is obligatory upon her to wear a *khimār*, and this is the garment that covers her head and chest. This is based upon the statement of the Prophet ﷺ:

لا يَقْبَلُ اللَّهُ صَلاةَ حَائِضٍ إِلاَّ بِخِمَارٍ.

"Allāh does not accept the prayer of a woman who reaches the age of

[26] *Ṣaḥīḥ Muslim* 517

menses, unless (she covers herself) with a *khimār* (overgarment)."[27]

Likewise, it is obligatory for her to cover her feet based upon the *ḥadīth*:

الْمَرْأَةُ عَوْرَةٌ.

"The woman is an *'awrah*."[28]

Umm Salamah was asked by the mother of Ibn Zayd concerning the garment of the woman during prayer. Umm Salamah said:

تُصَلِّي فِي الْخِمَارِ وَالدِّرْعِ السَّابِغِ الَّذِي يُغَيِّبُ ظُهُورَ قَدَمَيْهَا.

"She should pray in a *khimār* (head cover) and a long, loose fitting garment that covers the tops of her feet."[29]

This meaning is found in the *ḥadīth* of Umm Salamah:

قال رسول الله صلى الله عليه وسلم: من جر ثوبه خيلاء لم ينظر الله إليه يوم القيامة، فقالت أم سلمة: فكيف يصنعن النساء بذيولهن؟ قال: يرخين شبراً، فقالت: إذا تنكشف أقدامهن، قال: فيرخينه ذراعاً لا يزدن عليه.

"The Messenger of Allāh ﷺ said, 'Whoever allows his garment to drag out of pride, Allāh will not look at him on the Day of Resurrection.' Umm Salamah said, 'What should women do with their hems?' He said, 'Lower it a handspan.' She said, 'Then their feet will show.' He said, 'Let them lower it a cubit, but no more than that.'"[30]

---

[27] Narrated by Abū Dāwūd in *As-Salāh* (546); classed as *ṣaḥīḥ* by al-Albāni in *Ṣaḥīḥ Sunan Abī Dāwūd* (596).

[28] *Jāmi' at-Tirmidhī* 1173

[29] Narrated by Abū Dāwūd (639).

[30] Narrated by at-Tirmidhī (1731) and an-Nasā'ī (5336); classed as *ṣaḥīḥ* by al-Albāni in *Ṣaḥīḥ at-Tirmidhī*.

15. Walking in front of the person praying when they are leading the prayer or praying individually, and stepping over the people's necks during Friday prayer.

The person who walks in front of the person praying, or in front of his barrier, earns a sin. If the person is praying without a barrier, then he has up to the area he prostrates, and the person can walk beyond that.[31] The Prophet ﷺ said:

لَوْ يَعْلَمُ الْمَارُّ بَيْنَ يَدَيْ الْمُصَلِّي مَاذَا عَلَيْهِ لَكَانَ أَنْ يَقِفَ أَرْبَعِينَ خَيْرًا لَهُ مِنْ أَنْ يَمُرَّ بَيْنَ يَدَيْهِ.

"If the one who passes in front of a person who is praying knew what (a burden of sin) he bears, it would be better for him to stand for 40 rather than pass in front of him."[32]

Those who step over the necks of the people during Friday prayer harm the worshipers in addition to their tardiness for the prayer. It was narrated by 'Abdullāh bin Busr:

جَاءَ رَجُلٌ يَتَخَطَّى رِقَابَ النَّاسِ يَوْمَ الْجُمُعَةِ وَالنَّبِيُّ صَلَّى اللَّهُ عَلَيْهِ وَسَلَّمَ يَخْطُبُ، فَقَالَ لَهُ النَّبِيُّ صَلَّى اللَّهُ عَلَيْهِ وَسَلَّمَ: اجْلِسْ فَقَدْ آذَيْتَ.

"A man came and started stepping over the people one Friday when the Messenger of Allāh ﷺ was delivering the sermon, and the Prophet ﷺ said to him, 'Sit down, for you have annoyed (people).'"[33]

[31] Shaykh Ibn 'Uthaymeen رحمه الله said, concerning the differences of scholarly opinion concerning the distance within which the worshiper should stop anyone from passing in front of him: "The most correct opinion is that it is the distance between his feet and the place where he prostrates. That is because the one who is praying has no right to anything more than what he needs for his prayer. So he does not have the right to prevent the people from (using space) that he does not need." (*Ash-Sharh al-Mumti'* 3/340)

[32] Narrated by al-Bukhārī (510) and Muslim (507).

[33] Narrated by Abū Dāwūd (1118) and Ibn Mājah (1115).

Stepping over the people is prohibited. The person should sit in the *masjid* in the first open space, unless he sees a clear opening he can reach.

---

16. Not saying the opening *takbeer* when the person enters the prayer while the *imām* is in *rukoo'* (bowing).

This is a mistake because the opening *takbeer* is a pillar of the prayer; thus, it is obligatory for the person to say it while standing. Then after that, they bow with the *imām* in *rukoo'*. The opening *takbeer* suffices so the person does not need to say the *takbeer* for bowing into *rukoo'*, but if they begin with the opening *takbeer* and then say the *takbeer* for *rukoo'*, it is more complete. Abū Hurayrah ﵁ said:

أن النبي صلى الله عليه وسلم كان إِذَا قَامَ إِلَى الصَّلَاةِ يُكَبِّرُ حِينَ يَقُومُ ثُمَّ يُكَبِّرُ حِينَ يَرْكَعُ.

"When the Messenger of Allāh ﷺ stood up to pray, he would say *takbeer* when he stood up, then he would say *takbeer* when he bowed."[34]

---

17. Not following the *imām* when the person arrives while the *imām* is sitting or prostrating.

It is preferred and more correct for the person who enters the *masjid* to join the *imām* in any position he may be in, whether prostrating or otherwise. The Prophet ﷺ said:

إِذَا جِئْتُمْ إِلَى الصَّلاةِ وَنَحْنُ سُجُودٌ فَاسْجُدُوا.

"If you come to prayer and we are prostrating, then prostrate."[35]

---

[34] Narrated by al-Bukhārī (789) and Muslim (392).

[35] Narrated by Abū Dāwūd (893); classed as *hasan* by al-Albāni in *Ṣaḥīḥ Sunan Abī Dāwūd*.

If someone delays prostrating, he deprives himself of an act of worship that is beloved to Allāh. The Prophet ﷺ said:

إِذَا أَتَى أَحَدُكُمْ الصَّلاةَ وَالإِمَامُ عَلَى حَالٍ فَلْيَصْنَعْ كَمَا يَصْنَعُ الإِمَامُ.

"When one of you comes to the prayer and the *imām* is in any position, let him do what the *imām* is doing."[36]

Mu'ādh bin Jabal رضي الله عنه said:

لاَ أَرَاهُ عَلَى حَالٍ إِلاَّ كُنْتُ عَلَيْهَا. قَالَ فَقَالَ إِنَّ مُعَاذًا قَدْ سَنَّ لَكُمْ سُنَّةً كَذَلِكَ فَافْعَلُوا.

"I do not see him (the Prophet) in any position except that I follow him." The Prophet ﷺ said, "Surely, Mu'ādh has initiated a *sunnah* for you, so follow it.[37]

---

18. Actions that distract the person from the prayer.

This is proof that the person prefers the worldly life over the Hereafter, obeying his desire over obedience to Allāh, amusement over remembrance of Allāh, and that is a loss and evil consequence upon the individual. Allāh the Exalted said:

﴿ يَا أَيُّهَا الَّذِينَ آمَنُوا لَا تُلْهِكُمْ أَمْوَالُكُمْ وَلَا أَوْلَادُكُمْ عَن ذِكْرِ اللَّهِ ۚ وَمَن يَفْعَلْ ذَٰلِكَ فَأُولَٰئِكَ هُمُ الْخَاسِرُونَ ﴾

O you who believe! Let not your properties or your children divert you from the remembrance of Allāh. And whosoever does that, then they are the losers.

[Sūrah al-Munāfiqūn 63:9]

---

[36] Narrated by at-Tirmidhī (591); classed as *ṣaḥīḥ* by al-Albāni in *Ṣaḥīḥ at-Tirmidhī.*

[37] *Sunan Abī Dāwūd* 506

And He praised the believers with His statement:

﴿ رِجَالٌ لَّا تُلْهِيهِمْ تِجَارَةٌ وَلَا بَيْعٌ عَن ذِكْرِ اللَّهِ وَإِقَامِ الصَّلَاةِ ﴾

Men whom neither trade nor sale diverts them from the remembrance of Allāh, nor from establishing the prayer.

[Sūrah an-Nūr 24:37]

This is any action that distracts the person from prayer or causes them to be lazy in it, such as staying awake all night. This is not permissible because that which leads to the impermissible is, itself, impermissible. And Allāh guides to the Straight Path.

---

19. Fidgeting with clothes or watches during the prayer.

This action negates focus and devoutness in the prayer, and the proof for focus and devoutness in the prayer has been mentioned in the 5th affair. The Messenger of Allāh ﷺ forbade rubbing pebbles during the prayer because it negates focus in the prayer. He said:

إِذَا قَامَ أَحَدُكُمْ فِي الصَّلَاةِ فَلَا يَمْسَحِ الْحَصَى فَإِنَّ الرَّحْمَةَ تُوَاجِهُهُ.

"When one of you is standing in prayer, let him not rub pebbles, because the mercy of Allāh is facing him."[38]

The movement may increase to the extent that it no longer appears as though he is praying, and thus the prayer will be invalid.

---

20. Closing the eyes during the prayer without reason.

Closing the eyes during the prayer is hated. Ibn al-Qayyim رحمه الله said:

[38] *Sunan an-Nasā'ī* 1191

"Closing the eyes during the prayer is not from the guidance of the Prophet ﷺ. And the scholars have differed over whether it is hated or not. Imām Aḥmad and others have stated that this is hated. They said it resembles the action of the Jews, while other scholars have allowed it without hating it. They said: It could be more likely to bring about focus during the prayer, and focus and devoutness is the spirit, distinction, and intent of the prayer. The correct viewpoint is: If opening the eyes does not infringe on focusing in the prayer, then it is better. If opening the eyes comes between the person and focusing in the prayer due to something in front of him such as decoration, ornaments, or something that will distract his heart, then it is not hated to close the eyes at all. The viewpoint that, in this case, it is recommended to close the eyes, is closer to the principle of the legislation and the intent of the prayer than the statement that it is hated. And Allāh knows best."

---

21. Eating, drinking, and laughing during the prayer invalidates the prayer.

Eating and drinking during the obligatory prayers invalidates the prayer according to the consensus of the scholars. Ibn al-Mundhir said: "The scholars have agreed that the person is prohibited from eating and drinking, and all the scholars from whom knowledge is taken have agreed that whoever purposely eats or drinks during the obligatory prayer must repeat his prayer." Likewise, the consensus of the scholars that laughing invalidates the prayer has also been narrated by Ibn al-Mundhir.

---

22. Raising the voice with recitation and disturbing those around you.

It is recommended that the person should be able to hear himself while not reciting so loudly that he harms those reciting the Qur'ān or praying. 'Imrān bin Ḥuṣayn narrated:

أَنَّ رَسُولَ اللَّهِ صلى الله عليه وسلم صَلَّى الظُّهْرَ فَجَعَلَ رَجُلٌ يَقْرَأُ خَلْفَهُ بِسَبِّحِ اسْمَ رَبِّكَ الأَعْلَى فَلَمَّا انْصَرَفَ قَالَ أَيُّكُمْ قَرَأَأَوْ أَيُّكُمُ الْقَارِئُ فَقَالَ رَجُلٌ أَنَا. فَقَالَ قَدْ ظَنَنْتُ أَنَّ بَعْضَكُمْ خَالَجَنِيهَا.

"The Messenger of Allāh ﷺ prayed the Dhuhr prayer and a man behind him recited Sūrah al-A'lā. When he finished, [the Prophet] turned and said, 'Which one of you was reciting?' or 'Which one of you was the reciter?' A man responded, 'It was I.' The Prophet ﷺ said, 'I thought that some of you were disputing with me (concerning what I was reciting).'"[39]

The scholars have said that this statement of the Prophet ﷺ was his disapproval of this action.

Ibn Taymiyyah said: "Whoever recites the Qur'ān while the people are praying optional prayers, then he should not recite loudly as to distract them. The Prophet ﷺ came out to his Companions and they were praying with their voices raised. He said:

إِنَّ الْمُصَلِّيَ يُنَاجِي رَبَّهُ فَلْيَنْظُرْ بِمَا يُنَاجِيهِ بِهِ وَلاَ يَجْهَرْ بَعْضُكُمْ عَلَى بَعْضٍ بِالْقُرْآنِ.

"'When you pray, you are talking confidentially to your Lord. So look to what you confide to Him with, and do not raise your voices over each other with the Qur'ān.'[40]"

---

23. Annoying the worshipers by crowding them.

This is from the prohibited harms. The worshiper selects a space which is empty, unless he sees an opening he can easily reach without harming the people. It is prohibited to harm the people, especially

[39] *Ṣaḥīḥ Muslim* 398

[40] Narrated by Imām Aḥmad (4928).

during Friday prayers. The Prophet ﷺ said to the man who stepped over the people during Friday prayers, which was narrated by ʿAbdullāh bin Busr:

اجْلِسْ فَقَدْ آذَيْتَ.

"Sit down, for you have annoyed (people)."[41]

---

24. Not straightening the rows for prayer.

Allāh commanded us to establish the prayer.

﴿ وَأَقِيمُوا الصَّلَاةَ ﴾

And establish the prayer.

[Sūrah al-Baqarah 2:43]

And the Prophet ﷺ said:

سَوُّوا صُفُوفَكُمْ، فَإِنَّ تَسْوِيَةَ الصُّفُوفِ مِنْ إِقَامَةِ الصَّلاةِ.

"Straighten your rows, for straightening the rows is part of establishing prayer."[42]

And the Prophet ﷺ said:

لَتُسَوُّنَّ صُفُوفَكُمْ أَوْ لَيُخَالِفَنَّ اللَّهُ بَيْنَ وُجُوهِكُمْ.

"Make your rows straight or Allāh will cause discord among you."[43]

There are numerous *ahādeeth* which command and incite the straightening of the rows for prayer.

---

[41] Narrated by Abū Dāwūd (1118) and Ibn Mājah (1115).

[42] *Ṣaḥīḥ al-Bukhārī* 723

[43] *Ṣaḥīḥ al-Bukhārī* 717; *Ṣaḥīḥ Muslim* 436

25. Raising the feet off the ground while in *sujood* (prostration).

This is in opposition to what we have been commanded with. Ibn 'Abbās ﷺ said that the Prophet ﷺ said:

أُمِرْتُ أَنْ أَسْجُدَ عَلَى سَبْعٍ وَلاَ أَكُفَّ شَعَرًا وَلاَ ثَوْبًا.

"I have been commanded to prostrate on seven, but not to tuck up my hair or my garment."[44]

The Prophet ﷺ said:

أُمِرْتُ أَنْ أَسْجُدَ عَلَى سَبْعَةِ أَعْظُمٍ عَلَى الْجَبْهَةِ وَأَشَارَ بِيَدِهِ عَلَى أَنْفِهِ وَالْيَدَيْنِ وَالرُّكْبَتَيْنِ وَأَطْرَافِ الْقَدَمَيْنِ.

"I have been commanded to prostrate on seven bones: on the forehead," and he pointed to his nose, "and on the two hands, the two knees, and the toes of the two feet."[45]

The person is commanded to prostrate on his feet, and the most complete manner of doing this is with the toes facing towards the *qiblah*. The restriction is that he must place a part of each foot on the ground. If he lifts either foot, his prostration is not correct if it remains raised throughout his prostration.

26. Placing the right hand over the left hand and raising the hands to the neck.

This is in opposition to the Sunnah, because the Prophet ﷺ used to place his right hand over his left hand on his chest. The Sunnah is accomplished by placing the hands in the middle of the chest or below it, at the heart. This is because the heart is in the chest, based

[44] *Sunan Ibn Mājah* 934

[45] *Ṣaḥīḥ al-Bukhārī* 812; *Ṣaḥīḥ Muslim* 490

upon the statement of Allāh the Exalted.

﴿ وَلَٰكِن تَعْمَى الْقُلُوبُ الَّتِي فِي الصُّدُورِ ﴾

But it is the hearts which are in the breasts that grow blind.

[Sūrah al-Ḥajj 22:46]

Raising the hands to the neck is a mistake and in opposition to the Sunnah. That which has been narrated from 'Alī concerning the explanation of the verse:

﴿ فَصَلِّ لِرَبِّكَ وَانْحَرْ ﴾

Therefore, turn in prayer to your Lord and sacrifice (to Him only).

[Sūrah al-Kawthar 108:2]

This narration is weak and cannot be used as evidence for placing the hands at the neck.

---

27. Raising the hands at the time of *sujood* (prostration) or raising the hands from the position of *sujood*.

This is in opposition to the well-known Sunnah which has been narrated by most of the Companions who narrated which position the hands should be raised to. It is befitting to adhere to the well-known Sunnah except in the case when the students of knowledge are alone with each other. In this case, he can do what he deems most correct from the Sunnah which the general viewpoint of the scholars opposes. But as for when he is in front of the people, he should do what is well-known, known from the Sunnah, which most of the scholars are upon.

The well-known Sunnah which must be adhered to is that there are four places where the hands are raised:

1) At the opening *takbeer*

2) When bowing for *rukoo'*

3) After raising from *rukoo'*

4) After standing for the third *rak'ah*

Ibn 'Umar ﷺ said:

أَنَّ رَسُولَ اللَّهِ صَلَّى اللَّهُ عَلَيْهِ وَسَلَّمَ كَانَ يَرْفَعُ يَدَيْهِ حَذْوَ مَنْكِبَيْهِ إِذَا افْتَتَحَ الصَّلاَةَ، وَإِذَا كَبَّرَ لِلرُّكُوعِ، وَإِذَا رَفَعَ رَأْسَهُ مِنَ الرُّكُوعِ رَفَعَهُمَا كَذَلِكَ.

"The Messenger of Allāh ﷺ used to raise his hands to shoulder level when he started to pray, when he said *'Allāhu Akbar'* before bowing in *rukoo'*, and when he raised his head from *rukoo'*."[46]

In another narration, it states:

وَلاَ يَفْعَلُ ذَلِكَ حِينَ يَسْجُدُ وَلاَ حِينَ يَرْفَعُ رَأْسَهُ مِنَ السُّجُودِ.

"But he did not do that when he prostrated or when he raised his head from prostration."[47]

In a narration collected by Muslim, he said:

وَلاَ يَفْعَلُهُ حِينَ يَرْفَعُ رَأْسَهُ مِنَ السُّجُودِ.

"But he did not do it at the time of raising his head from prostration."[48]

And Ibn 'Umar ﷺ said:

كَانَ رَسُولُ اللَّهِ صلى الله عليه وسلم إِذَا قَامَ مِنَ الرَّكْعَتَيْنِ كَبَّرَ وَرَفَعَ يَدَيْهِ.

---

[46] *Ṣaḥīḥ al-Bukhārī* 735; *Ṣaḥīḥ Muslim* 390

[47] *Sunan an-Nasā'ī* 876

[48] *Ṣaḥīḥ Muslim* 390

"When the Messenger of Allāh ﷺ stood at the end of two *raka'āt*, he uttered the *takbeer* ('Allāh is the Greatest') and raised his hands."[49]

---

28. Some of the *imāms* rush through the prayer without tranquility and without giving those following them the ability to become tranquil in the prayer and recite Sūrah al-Fātihah, especially in the final *rak'ah*.

The *imām* is responsible for having a good, sound prayer because the people take him as an example, so it is upon him to investigate and study the Sunnah. Tranquility is a pillar of the prayer, and it is even more affirmed as it relates to the *imām* because he is followed as an example. Likewise, reciting al-Fātihah is a pillar of the prayer, so it is obligatory that those following the *imām* be given the opportunity to recite it. We have already mentioned the proof for tranquility and the recitation of al-Fātihah being pillars of the prayer.

---

29. Not giving concern to prostrating upon seven bones (the forehead with the nose, the two palms, the two knees, and the toes of both feet).

Al-'Abbās bin 'Abdil-Muttalib ﷺ said, "I heard the Messenger of Allāh ﷺ say:

إِذَا سَجَدَ الْعَبْدُ سَجَدَ مَعَهُ سَبْعَةُ آرَابٍ وَجْهُهُ وَكَفَّاهُ وَرُكْبَتَاهُ وَقَدَمَاهُ.

"'When a person prostrates, seven parts of his body prostrate with him: his forehead, his two hands, his two knees, and his two feet.'"[50]

Ibn 'Abbās ﷺ said that the Prophet ﷺ said:

أُمِرْتُ أَنْ أَسْجُدَ عَلَى سَبْعَةِ أَعْظُمٍ عَلَى الْجَبْهَةِ وَأَشَارَ بِيَدِهِ عَلَى أَنْفِهِ

[49] *Sunan Abī Dāwūd* 743

[50] *Ṣaḥīḥ Muslim* 491

وَالْيَدَيْنِ وَالرُّكْبَتَيْنِ وَأَطْرَافِ الْقَدَمَيْنِ.

"I have been commanded to prostrate on seven bones: on the forehead," and he pointed to his nose, "and on the two hands, the two knees, and the toes of the two feet."[51]

There are some people who don't place the forehead and nose firmly upon the ground when in *sujood*, or they lift their feet, or they don't place their palms firmly on the ground. All of this contradicts what we have been commanded to do.

---

30. Not giving concern to learning the rules and regulations of the prayer

This opposes the manner in which the Muslims should conduct themselves, for surely the prayer is the greatest physical pillar of Islām. Allāh has commanded us to establish the prayer:

﴿ وَأَقِيمُوا الصَّلَاةَ ﴾

And establish the prayer.

[Sūrah al-Baqarah 2:43]

There are 70 verses or more containing this command, and it is not possible to establish the prayer without knowing its rules and regulations and knowing the manner of the Prophet's prayer ﷺ. The prayer is from the actions of which no one is allowed to be ignorant. Its rulings must be known, as well as its conditions, pillars, obligations, and its rulings for the prostration of forgetfulness and the like. It is obligatory to know these rulings. Not knowing these rulings could cause the Muslim to be ignorant of what invalidates his prayer. And Allāh is the One Who guides and grants success.

---

[51] *Ṣaḥīḥ al-Bukhārī* 812; *Ṣaḥīḥ Muslim* 490

31–34. Not giving concern to the recitation of al-Fātihah and reciting it with errors. An example of this is reciting the word *'ālamīn* with a *kasrah* vowel on the letter *lam,* placing a *fatḥah* vowel on the letter *hamzah* in the word *ihdina*, and placing a *ḍammah* vowel on the letter *taa'* in the word *an'amta*.

These mistakes and mistakes similar to these must be avoided, and the person who makes mistakes like this cannot lead others in prayer. If he makes a mistake that alters the meaning of the verse—such as placing a *ḍammah* vowel on the letter *taa'* in the word *an'amta*—his prayer is invalid.

---

35. Cracking the knuckles.

This is hated and prohibited during the prayer. As for cracking the knuckles, it has been narrated that Shu'bah, the freed slave of Ibn 'Abbas, said:

صليت إلى جنب ابن عباس ففقّعت أصابعي، فلما قضيت الصلاة قال: لا أمَّ لك ! تفقع أصابعك وأنت في الصلاة.

"May you have no mother![52] You crack your knuckles while you are praying?"[53]

---

36. Interlocking the fingers.

This is hated. The Prophet ﷺ said:

إِذَا تَوَضَّأَ أَحَدُكُمْ فَأَحْسَنَ وُضُوءَهُ ثُمَّ خَرَجَ عَامِدًا إِلَى الْمَسْجِدِ فَلا

[52] **Translator's note:** 'Iyāḍ said: "This is a normal saying of the Arab when displeased or amazed by something and the actual meaning of the statement is not intended. (*Explanation of Ṣaḥīḥ al-Bukhārī*)

[53] Narrated by Ibn Abī Shaybah (2/344). Al-Albāni reported it in *Irwa' al-Ghaleel* (2/99).

يُشَبِّكَنَّ يَدَيْهِ، فَإِنَّهُ فِي صَلاةٍ.

"When one of you performs *wudoo'* and does it well, then goes out intending the *masjid*, let him not interlace his hands, for he is in a state of prayer."

Abū Hurayrah ﷺ said, "The Prophet ﷺ said:

إِذَا تَوَضَّأَ أَحَدُكُمْ فِي بَيْتِهِ ثُمَّ أَتَى الْمَسْجِدَ كَانَ فِي صَلَاةٍ حَتَّى يَرْجِعَ فَلَا يَفْعَلُ هَكَذَا، وَشَبَّكَ بَيْنَ أَصَابِعِهِ.

"'When one of you performs *wudoo'* in his home then goes to the *masjid,* he is in prayer until he returns, thus let him not do like this.' And he interlocked his fingers."

---

37. Putting someone forward to lead the prayer who is not qualified while more qualified people are present.

This opposes the purpose of the *imām*. And he is an example, thus the *imām* must be one of understanding who is able to recite. The Prophet ﷺ said:

يَؤُمُّ الْقَوْمَ أَقْرَؤُهُمْ لِكِتَابِ اللَّهِ.

"Put forth those best versed in the recitation of the Book of Allāh to lead the prayer."[54]

The scholars have affirmed that the person who does not recite well should not be put forward to lead the prayer, nor the person with obvious sin upon him, or the person with a bad history, or the innovator, or the sinner and the like. They are not to be put forward. But if they are put forward to lead the prayer, the prayer of those praying behind them is correct. And Allāh knows best.

---

[54] *Ṣaḥīḥ Muslim* 2373

38. Grammatical mistakes in the recitation of the Noble Qur'ān.

This is an obvious deficiency. It is the right of the Qur'ān that it be recited free of grammatical errors. Thus, the Muslim strives with himself to recite with *tajweed* and a good recitation. Allāh the Exalted said:

﴿ وَرَتِّلِ الْقُرْآنَ تَرْتِيلًا ﴾

And recite the Qur'ān (aloud) in a slow, (pleasant tone and) style.

[Sūrah al-Muzzammil 73:4]

And He said:

﴿ فَإِذَا قَرَأْنَاهُ فَاتَّبِعْ قُرْآنَهُ ﴾

And when We have recited it to you, then follow you its recital.

[Sūrah al-Qiyāmah 75:18]

The meaning of that is to recite it with the proper vowelization it deserves, pronouncing the letters clearly, without grammatical errors. There is a reward for the person who does this with a sincere intention. 'Ā'ishah رضي الله عنها said that the Prophet ﷺ said:

الماهِرُ بالقرآنِ؛ مع السَّفَرَةِ الكِرامِ البررة، والذي يَقرأ القرآنَ ويَتَتَعْتَعُ فيه وهو عليه شاقٌّ؛ له أجْرانِ.

"The one who is skilled in reciting Qur'ān will be with the noble and obedient scribes (i.e., the angels), and the one who reads the Qur'ān and struggles with it because it is difficult for him will have two rewards."[55]

[55] *Ṣaḥīḥ Muslim* 798

39. Some men praying behind the women in Masjid al-Ḥarām.

This includes men praying behind women in other places as well. This is from the hated things in the prayer because it is the Sunnah for the women to pray behind the men. When men pray behind women, it removes focus and devotion from their prayers and it distracts from their prayer due to them looking at [the women]. Men should never line up to pray behind women except when it is unavoidable, like those who end up behind women because they missed the Eid or Jumu'ah prayer. Some of the scholars have stated that the exception for this is when praying in Masjid al-Harām. This was stated by Shaykh 'Abdul-'Azeez bin Baz رَحِمَهُ ٱللَّهُ.

40. Women coming to the *masjid* beautified and perfumed.

This is an obvious evil witnessed during Ramaḍān and outside of Ramaḍān. The woman is only coming to the prayer to worship her Guardian, not to display her beauty and clothes. Perhaps men will look at her, so she will earn a sin and decrease her reward based upon her action.

The Prophet ﷺ said:

أَيُّمَا امْرَأَةٍ أَصَابَتْ بَخُورًا فَلاَ تَشْهَدْ مَعَنَا الْعِشَاءَ الآخِرَةَ.

"Any woman who has scented herself with *bakhoor* (incense), let her not attend 'Ishā' prayers with us."[56]

The Prophet ﷺ said:

لَا تَمْنَعُوا إِمَاءَ اللَّهِ مَسَاجِدَ اللَّهِ وَلَكِنْ لِيَخْرُجْنَ وَهُنَّ تَفِلَاتٌ.

"Do not prevent the female servants of Allāh from going to the

[56] *Ṣaḥīḥ Muslim* 444

mosques of Allāh, but let them go out looking unadorned."[57]

The meaning of "unadorned" is not beautified and not perfumed.

[57] Narrated by Aḥmad (9362) and Abū Dāwūd (565).

6

Mistakes Related to *Du'ā'*

1. Raising the hands after the obligatory prayers.

If the person adheres to this practice, it is an innovation. After the obligatory prayers, the Sunnah is to remember Allāh, seek forgiveness, say "nothing has the right to be worshiped except Allāh, Allāh is free from imperfections, all praises belong to Allāh, Allāh is the Greatest," and to supplicate individually without raising the hands. This is what the Prophet ﷺ used to do. He did not raise his hands in *du'ā'* after the obligatory prayers. To do so is in opposition to the Sunnah, and adhering to this practice is an innovation.

2. Raising the hands during the obligatory prayers.

This is like the person who raises his hands as he is rising from bowing, as though he is supplicating in *qunoot*. This has not been narrated from the Sunnah of the Prophet ﷺ, and this was not done by the rightly guided caliphs, nor was it done by any of the Companions. And any action not done by the Prophet ﷺ and his Companions falls into his statement:

مَنْ أَحْدَثَ فِي أَمْرِنَا هَذَا مَا لَيْسَ مِنْهُ فَهُوَ رَدٌّ.

"Whoever introduces something into this affair of ours which is not from it, it is rejected."[1]

مَنْ عَمِلَ عَمَلاً لَيْسَ عَلَيْهِ أَمْرُنَا فَهُوَ رَدٌّ.

"Whoever does an action which is not from our affair, it is rejected."[2]

---

3. Apathy as it relates to focus and an attentive heart during *du'ā'*.

Allāh the Exalted said:

﴿ ادْعُوا رَبَّكُمْ تَضَرُّعًا وَخُفْيَةً ﴾

Invoke your Lord with humility and in secret.

[Sūrah al-A'rāf 7:55]

And Allāh the Exalted said:

﴿ إِنَّهُمْ كَانُوا يُسَارِعُونَ فِي الْخَيْرَاتِ وَيَدْعُونَنَا رَغَبًا وَرَهَبًا ۖ وَكَانُوا لَنَا خَاشِعِينَ ﴾

Verily, they used to hasten to do good deeds, and they used to call on Us with hope and fear, and used to humble themselves before Us.

[Sūrah al-Anbiyā' 21:90]

When supplicating, the person must have focus, humility, humbleness, and an attentive heart. These are the manners of *du'ā'*. The person who supplicates is diligent in receiving an answer to his *du'ā'* and having his request fulfilled; it is a must that he is diligent in

[1] *Ṣaḥīḥ Muslim* 1718

[2] *Ṣaḥīḥ Muslim* 1718

perfecting his *du'ā'* and adorning it so that it is elevated to his Creator such that He will answer it.

The Prophet ﷺ said:

ادْعُوا اللَّهَ وَأَنْتُمْ مُوقِنُونَ بِالْإِجَابَةِ، وَاعْلَمُوا أَنَّ اللَّهَ لَا يَسْتَجِيبُ دُعَاءً مِنْ قَلْبٍ غَافِلٍ لَاهٍ.

"Call upon Allāh while you are certain of a response, and remember that Allāh will not answer a *du'ā'* that comes from a negligent and heedless heart."[3]

---

4. Losing hope that the *du'ā'* will be accepted and being hasty waiting for a response.

This is from the affairs which prevent *du'ā'* from being accepted. The Prophet ﷺ said:

يُسْتَجَابُ لأَحَدِكُمْ مَا لَمْ يَعْجَلْ يَقُولُ دَعَوْتُ فَلَمْ يُسْتَجَبْ لِي.

"The *du'ā'* of one of you will be accepted as long as he is not hasty and doesn't say, 'I supplicated but I was not answered.'"[4]

We have previously mentioned that the person must be certain his *du'ā'* will be answered because he is supplicating to the Most Kind and Most Generous. Allāh the Exalted said:

﴿وَقَالَ رَبُّكُمُ ادْعُونِي أَسْتَجِبْ لَكُمْ﴾

And your Lord said, "Invoke Me, I will respond to your (invocation)."

[Sūrah Ghāfir 40:60]

---

[3] Narrated by at-Tirmidhī (3479); classed as *hasan* by Shaykh al-Albāni in *Ṣaḥīḥ at-Tirmidhī* (2766).

[4] *Ṣaḥīḥ al-Bukhārī* 6340

The person whose supplication is not accepted must fall into one of two categories:

1) There are things present preventing his supplication from being answered, such as breaking the ties of kinship, wrongdoing, or consuming that which is impermissible. In most cases, this will prevent the *du'ā'* from being answered.

2) The answer to his *du'ā'* will be delayed and stored for him or an evil will be diverted from him equivalent to his supplication. The Prophet ﷺ said:

مَا مِنْ مُسْلِمٍ يَدْعُو بِدَعْوَةٍ لَيْسَ فِيهَا إِثْمٌ، وَلَا قَطِيعَةُ رَحِمٍ، إِلَّا أَعْطَاهُ اللهُ بِهَا إِحْدَى ثَلَاثٍ: إِمَّا أَنْ تُعَجَّلَ لَهُ دَعْوَتُهُ، وَإِمَّا أَنْ يَدَّخِرَهَا لَهُ فِي الْآخِرَةِ، وَإِمَّا أَنْ يَصْرِفَ عَنْهُ مِنَ السُّوءِ مِثْلَهَا . قَالُوا: إِذًا نُكْثِرُ . قَالَ: اللهُ أَكْثَرُ.

"There is no Muslim who calls upon his Lord with a *du'ā'* in which there is no sin or severing of family ties except that Allāh will give him one of three things: either He will answer his prayer quickly, or He will store (the reward for) it in the Hereafter, or He will divert an equivalent evil away from him." They said, "We will say more *du'ā'*." He said, "Allāh's bounty is greater."[5]

As for what has been narrated:

توسلوا بجاهي، فإن جاهي عند الله عظيم.

"Seek to draw closer to Allāh by virtue of my status, for my status with Allāh is great."[6]

This is a fabrication and it is not authentically narrated from the Prophet ﷺ.

---

[5] Narrated by Aḥmad (10749) and at-Tirmidhī (3573). Classed as *ṣaḥīḥ* by al-Albāni in *Mishkāt al-Masābeeh* (2199).

[6] **Translator's note:** Ibn Taymiyyah and al-Albāni said: It has no basis. See *Iqtidā' as-Sirāt al-Mustaqeem* by Ibn Taymiyyah (2/415) and *As-Silsilah ad-Da'eefah* (22) by al-Albāni.

5. Overstepping the bounds in *du'ā'*, such as praying for something sinful or severing the ties of kinship.

This is from the matters which prevent *du'ā'* from being accepted. The Prophet ﷺ said:

سَيَكُونُ قَوْمٌ يَعْتَدُونَ فِي الدُّعَاءِ.

"There will be a people who exceed the bounds in *du'ā'*."[7]

Allāh the Exalted said:

﴿ ادْعُوا رَبَّكُمْ تَضَرُّعًا وَخُفْيَةً ۚ إِنَّهُ لَا يُحِبُّ الْمُعْتَدِينَ ﴾

Invoke your Lord with humility and in secret. He likes not the aggressors.

[Sūrah al-A'rāf 7:55]

Exceeding the bounds in *du'ā'* includes praying for something sinful, a calamity, or severing ties of kinship. The Prophet ﷺ said:

مَا عَلَى الأَرْضِ مُسْلِمٌ يَدْعُو اللَّهَ بِدَعْوَةٍ إِلاَّ آتَاهُ اللَّهُ إِيَّاهَا أَوْ صَرَفَ عَنْهُ مِنَ السُّوءِ مِثْلَهَا مَا لَمْ يَدْعُ بِمَأْثَمٍ أَوْ قَطِيعَةِ رَحِمٍ.

"There is not a Muslim upon the earth who calls upon Allāh with any supplication except that Allāh grants it to him or He turns away from him the like of it in evil, as long as he does not supplicate for something sinful or for severing the ties of kinship."[8]

---

[7] *Sunan Ibn Mājah* 3864

[8] *Jāmi' at-Tirmidhī* 3573

7

Mistakes Concerning Jumu'ah (Friday)

1. Specifying the night of Jumu'ah with the night prayer and the day of Jumu'ah with fasting.

This is prohibited based upon the narration of Muḥammad bin Ubad bin Ja'far, who said:

سَأَلْتُ جَابِرًا رضي الله عنه: أَنَهَى رَسُولُ اللَّهِ صَلَّى اللَّهُ عَلَيْهِ وَسَلَّمَ عَنْ صِيَامِ يَوْمِ الْجُمُعَةِ ؟ فَقَالَ: نَعَمْ.

"I asked Jābir ؓ, 'Did the Prophet ﷺ forbid fasting on Fridays?' He replied: 'Yes.'"[1]

The Prophet ﷺ said:

لا تَخْتَصُّوا لَيْلَةَ الْجُمُعَةِ بِقِيَامٍ مِنْ بَيْنِ اللَّيَالِي، وَلا تَخُصُّوا يَوْمَ الْجُمُعَةِ بِصِيَامٍ مِنْ بَيْنِ الأَيَّامِ، إلا أَنْ يَكُونَ فِي صَوْمٍ يَصُومُهُ أَحَدُكُمْ.

---

[1] Al-Bukhārī and Muslim

"Do not single out the night of Friday from other nights for standing in prayer, and do not single out Friday from other days for fasting, unless it is part of a fast that one of you regularly observes."[2]

---

2. Indifference towards listening to the Friday sermon, or talking while the *imām* is delivering the sermon.

Listening to the Friday sermon and remaining silent has been affirmed in many *aḥādīth,* as well as the prohibition of speaking and not listening to the sermon. The Prophet ﷺ said:

إِذَا قُلْتَ لِصَاحِبِكَ يَوْمَ الْجُمُعَةِ أَنْصِتْ. وَالإِمَامُ يَخْطُبُ فَقَدْ لَغَوْتَ.

"If you say to your companion when the *imām* is preaching on Friday, 'Listen attentively,' then you have engaged in idle talk."[3]

The statement "listen attentively" interrupts the *imām*, even though the interruption is slight, thus it results in idle talk. This is as it relates to the person who gives advice to the one talking, so how about the person who initiates the conversation?! Al-Ḥafiẓ said in his explanation of *Ṣaḥīḥ al-Bukhārī*: "If the statement 'listen attentively'—even though it is enjoining the good—is considered idle talk, then every other type of speech is more befitting to be labeled idle talk."

---

3. Buying and selling after the second *adhān* (call to prayer).

Buying and selling is not permissible after the *adhān*, and this transaction is invalid based upon the statement of Allāh the Exalted:

﴿ يَا أَيُّهَا الَّذِينَ آمَنُوا إِذَا نُودِيَ لِلصَّلَاةِ مِن يَوْمِ الْجُمُعَةِ
فَاسْعَوْا إِلَىٰ ذِكْرِ اللَّهِ وَذَرُوا الْبَيْعَ ۚ ذَٰلِكُمْ خَيْرٌ لَّكُمْ إِن

---

[2] *Ṣaḥīḥ Muslim* 1144

[3] *Ṣaḥīḥ al-Bukhārī* 892; *Ṣaḥīḥ Muslim* 851

﴿ كُنتُمْ تَعْلَمُونَ ﴾

O you who believe! When the call is proclaimed for the prayer on the day of Friday (Jumu'ah prayer), come to the remembrance of Allāh and leave off business; that is better for you, if you did but know!

[Sūrah al-Jumu'ah 62:9]

Trade is prohibited after the *adhān*—meaning the second *adhān*—and the transaction at this time is invalid, because the prohibition necessitates it being invalid.

---

4. Praying after the *adhān* when the *imām* enters; this is what the commoners call "the Sunnah prayers of Jumu'ah."

This prayer is not the Sunnah and it was not done by the Messenger of Allāh ﷺ. Ibn al-Qayyim رحمه الله said, "After Bilāl completed calling the *adhān,* the Prophet ﷺ began delivering the sermon and no one stood and prayed two *raka'āt*, ever. And there was only one *adhān*. This is proof that Jumu'ah prayer is similar to the Eid prayer; there are no Sunnah prayers before it. This is the most correct statement of the scholars and this is proven by the Sunnah."

Then he said: "Those who think that when Bilāl رضي الله عنه completed calling the *adhān*, all of the Companions stood and prayed two *raka'āt*, then they are the most ignorant people of the Sunnah. This is what proves that there are no Sunnah prayers before Jumu'ah. This is the *madh'hab* of Mālik and Aḥmad and one of the views of the companions of Shāfi'ī."

---

5. Stepping over the people.

This is a prevalent mistake and it harms those worshipers who arrived early. A *ḥadīth* has been narrated by 'Abdullāh bin Busr prohibiting this. He said:

جَاءَ رَجُلٌ يَتَخَطَّى رِقَابَ النَّاسِ يَوْمَ الْجُمُعَةِ وَالنَّبِيُّ صَلَّى اللَّهُ عَلَيْهِ وَسَلَّمَ يَخْطُبُ، فَقَالَ لَهُ النَّبِيُّ صَلَّى اللَّهُ عَلَيْهِ وَسَلَّمَ: اجْلِسْ فَقَدْ آذَيْتَ.

"A man came and started stepping over the people one Friday when the Messenger of Allāh ﷺ was delivering the sermon, and the Prophet ﷺ said to him: 'Sit down, for you have annoyed (people).'"[4]

---

6. Prolonging the sermon while shortening the prayer.

This opposes the Sunnah. The Sunnah is to shorten the sermon, making it straightforward with no filler, while lengthening the prayer. 'Abdullāh bin Abī Awfa said:

كَانَ رَسُولُ اللَّهِ صلى الله عليه وسلم يُطِيلُ الصَّلاَةَ وَيُقَصِّرُ الْخُطْبَةَ.

"The Messenger of Allāh ﷺ used to make the prayer long while keeping the sermon short."[5]

'Ammār bin Yāsir ﷺ said, "I heard the Messenger of Allāh ﷺ say:

إِنَّ طُولَ صَلاَةِ الرَّجُلِ وَقِصَرَ خُطْبَتِهِ مَئِنَّةٌ مِنْ فِقْهِهِ فَأَطِيلُوا الصَّلاَةَ وَاقْصُرُوا الْخُطْبَةَ وَإِنَّ مِنَ الْبَيَانِ سِحْرًا.

"'A man's lengthening his prayer and shortening his sermon is a sign of his understanding (of religion), so make your prayers lengthy and your sermon brief, for there is some eloquent speech which is magic.'"[6]

This *ḥadīth* comprises a command to lengthen the prayer and shorten the sermon; it combines his statement, his action, and his command.

---

[4] Narrated by Abū Dāwūd (1118) and Ibn Mājah (1115).

[5] *Sunan an-Nasā'ī*

[6] *Ṣaḥīḥ Muslim* 969

7. Touching stones or fidgeting with *dhikr* beads and the like.

This is prohibited. This includes fidgeting with the *ghutrah* (traditional headscarf for men), clothes, the *masjid* carpet, *miswak*, or something else like prayer beads, a watch, or a pen. This is prohibited based upon the *ḥadīth* collected in *Ṣaḥīḥ Muslim*. The Prophet ﷺ said:

مَنْ تَوَضَّأَ فَأَحْسَنَ الْوُضُوءَ ثُمَّ أَتَى الْجُمُعَةَ فَاسْتَمَعَ وَأَنْصَتَ غُفِرَ لَهُ مَا بَيْنَهُ وَبَيْنَ الْجُمُعَةِ وَزِيَادَةُ ثَلاثَةِ أَيَّامٍ وَمَنْ مَسَّ الْحَصَى فَقَدْ لَغَا.

"Whoever performs *wudoo'* and does *wudoo'* well, then comes to Jumu'ah and listens attentively, will be forgiven (his sins) between that and (the next) Jumu'ah, and three days in addition to that; but whoever touches the pebbles has engaged in an idle action."[7]

8. Singling out Jumu'ah to observe fasting.

There are numerous narrations prohibiting singling out Jumu'ah for fasting. Abū Hurayrah ﷺ said, "I heard the Messenger of Allāh ﷺ say:

لا يَصُومَنَّ أَحَدُكُمْ يَوْمَ الْجُمُعَةِ إِلا يَوْمًا قَبْلَهُ أَوْ بَعْدَهُ.

"'None of you should fast on a Friday unless he fasts the day before or the day after.'"[8]

And the Prophet ﷺ said:

لا تَخُصُّوا يَوْمَ الْجُمُعَةِ بِصِيَامٍ مِنْ بَيْنِ الأَيَّامِ، إِلا أَنْ يَكُونَ فِي صَوْمٍ يَصُومُهُ أَحَدُكُمْ.

[7] *Ṣaḥīḥ Muslim* 875

[8] *Ṣaḥīḥ al-Bukhārī* 1849; *Ṣaḥīḥ Muslim* 1929

"Do not single out Friday from other days for fasting, unless it is part of a fast that one of you regularly observes."[9]

Likewise, there is a prohibition for singling out Friday for fasting in the *ḥadīth* of Juwayriyyah bint al-Harith ﵂, the wife of the Prophet ﷺ:

أَنَّ النَّبِيَّ صلى الله عليه وسلم دَخَلَ عَلَيْهَا يَوْمَ الْجُمُعَةِ وَهْىَ صَائِمَةٌ فَقَالَ أَصُمْتِ أَمْسِ. قَالَتْ لاَ. قَالَ تُرِيدِينَ أَنْ تَصُومِي غَدًا. قَالَتْ لاَ. قَالَ فَأَفْطِرِي.

The Prophet ﷺ visited her on a Friday and she was fasting. He asked her, "Did you fast yesterday?" She said, "No." He said, "Do you intend to fast tomorrow?" She said, "No." He said, "Then break your fast."[10]

There are many narrations that prohibit this. And the wisdom for this prohibition—and Allāh knows best—is what was mentioned by Ibn al-Qayyim ﵀ in his statement: "This is to block the path of attributing something to the religion which is not from it. And this would necessitate imitating the disbelievers in specifying certain days to take off from worldly work. Added to this is the fact that the virtue of this day (Friday) over other days is well-known, so the call to fast on this day is strong. Thus, it is presumed that this will lead the people to fast on this day and celebrate it in a manner in which other days are not celebrated. Consequently, they will attach something to the religion which is not from it."

---

[9] *Ṣaḥīḥ Muslim* 1144

[10] *Ṣaḥīḥ al-Bukhārī* 1986

8

Mistakes Related to *Zakāh* (Charity)

---

1. Apathy towards *zakāh* or being lackadaisical towards paying it on time.

This is evil and a clear sin because *zakāh* is the third pillar of Islām and a right upon the wealth. Thus, it is obligatory upon the Muslim to pay it within the appropriate time period, while enjoying doing so, seeking to draw close to his Guardian (Allāh). Allāh has threatened those who refuse to pay *zakāh*, with a severe threat—may Allāh save us from it. Allāh the Exalted said:

﴿ وَلَا يَحْسَبَنَّ الَّذِينَ يَبْخَلُونَ بِمَا آتَاهُمُ اللَّهُ مِن فَضْلِهِ
هُوَ خَيْرًا لَّهُم ۖ بَلْ هُوَ شَرٌّ لَّهُمْ ۖ سَيُطَوَّقُونَ مَا بَخِلُوا بِهِ
يَوْمَ الْقِيَامَةِ ۗ وَلِلَّهِ مِيرَاثُ السَّمَاوَاتِ وَالْأَرْضِ ۗ وَاللَّهُ بِمَا
تَعْمَلُونَ خَبِيرٌ ﴾

And let not those who covetously withhold of that which Allāh has bestowed on them of His Bounty (wealth) think that it is good for them. Nay, it will be worse for them; the things which they covetously withheld shall be tied to their necks like a collar on the Day of Resurrection. And to Allāh belongs the heritage of the heavens and the earth; and Allāh is Well-Acquainted with all that you do.

[Sūrah Āli 'Imrān 3:180]

The Messenger of Allāh ﷺ said:

مَا مِنْ صَاحِبِ ذَهَبٍ وَلَا فِضَّةٍ لَا يُؤَدِّي مِنْهَا حَقَّهَا إِلَّا إِذَا كَانَ يَوْمُ الْقِيَامَةِ صُفِّحَتْ لَهُ صَفَائِحَ مِنْ نَارٍ فَأُحْمِيَ عَلَيْهَا فِي نَارِ جَهَنَّمَ فَيُكْوَى بِهَا جَنْبُهُ وَجَبِينُهُ وَظَهْرُهُ كُلَّمَا بَرَدَتْ أُعِيدَتْ لَهُ فِي يَوْمٍ كَانَ مِقْدَارُهُ خَمْسِينَ أَلْفَ سَنَةٍ حَتَّى يُقْضَى بَيْنَ الْعِبَادِ.

"There is no owner of gold or silver who does not pay what is due on it (*zakāh*) except that when the Day of Resurrection comes, plates of fire will be prepared for him from the Hellfire, and they will brand his forehead, his flanks, and his back, and every time they cool down they will be reheated, on a Day the length of which is equal to fifty thousand years, until judgment is passed among the people."[1]

And Allāh says:

﴿ وَالَّذِينَ يَكْنِزُونَ الذَّهَبَ وَالْفِضَّةَ وَلَا يُنفِقُونَهَا فِي سَبِيلِ اللَّهِ فَبَشِّرْهُم بِعَذَابٍ أَلِيمٍ ﴿٣٤﴾ يَوْمَ يُحْمَىٰ عَلَيْهَا فِي نَارِ جَهَنَّمَ فَتُكْوَىٰ بِهَا جِبَاهُهُمْ وَجُنُوبُهُمْ وَظُهُورُهُمْ ۖ هَٰذَا مَا كَنَزْتُمْ لِأَنفُسِكُمْ فَذُوقُوا مَا كُنتُمْ تَكْنِزُونَ ﴿٣٥﴾ ﴾

And those who hoard up gold and silver, and spend it not in the cause of Allāh; announce unto them a painful torment. On the Day when it will be heated in the Fire of Hell and it will be branded on their foreheads, their flanks, and their backs, (and it will

[1] *Ṣaḥīḥ Muslim* 987

> be said unto them): "This is the treasure which you hoarded for yourselves. Now taste of what you used to hoard."
>
> *[Sūrah at-Tawbah 9:34-35]*

The time for paying *zakāh* on wealth, and that which falls upon the same ruling, is after one lunar year passes. Thus, each year the Muslim purifies his wealth if his wealth has reached the *nisab*[2]. He searches for those within the eight categories of people able to receive the *zakāh*. It is not permissible for him to delay paying the *zakāh* past its proper time, except if he has a valid reason supported by Islamic legislation. And Allāh knows best.

---

2. Not showing concerning for knowing the rules and regulations of *zakāh*, having apathy towards learning the wealth on which *zakāh* is due, and having apathy towards paying *zakāh* in its proper time.

It is obligatory for the person with wealth to learn or ask about *zakāh* because it is an obligation upon him. And he will not pay it in the prescribed manner unless he learns the rules and regulations as it relates to the *nisab*, the type of wealth, the amount of *zakāh*, and the paths in which it is given.

The person who is lackadaisical is learning these matters will perhaps fall into prohibited matters without knowledge or earn a sin by delaying the *zakāh*, or by not giving it to those who truly deserve it. *Zakāh* is an obligation upon the wealth. In order to pay *zakāh* in the manner which fulfills the obligation, the person must acquire knowledge, either by studying or asking.

[2] **Translator's note:** *Nisab* is the minimum amount for a Muslim's net worth in order for him to be obligated to give charity.

3. Being careless in regard to giving *zakāh* to those who deserve it.

Allāh the Exalted said:

﴿ إِنَّمَا الصَّدَقَاتُ لِلْفُقَرَاءِ وَالْمَسَاكِينِ وَالْعَامِلِينَ عَلَيْهَا وَالْمُؤَلَّفَةِ قُلُوبُهُمْ وَفِي الرِّقَابِ وَالْغَارِمِينَ وَفِي سَبِيلِ اللَّهِ وَابْنِ السَّبِيلِ ۖ فَرِيضَةً مِّنَ اللَّهِ ۗ وَاللَّهُ عَلِيمٌ حَكِيمٌ ﴾

Charity (*zakāh*) is only for the *fuqara'* (poor), and *al-masakin* (the poor), and those employed to collect (the funds); and to attract the hearts of those who have been inclined (towards Islām); and to free the captives; and for those in debt; and for Allāh's cause, and for the wayfarer; a duty imposed by Allāh. And Allāh is All-Knower, All-Wise.

[Sūrah at-Tawbah 9:60]

These are the eight categories of those who can receive *zakāh*. Those who are unconcerned about *zakāh,* so they don't give it to someone within these eight categories, then the money he gives is not considered *zakāh*. And he has not fulfilled his obligation.

There are some people who give *zakāh* to anyone, even if the person has enough to suffice him. They do not search for the poor or the others who can receive *zakāh* from the eight categories. This is because they are too lazy to search out the poor and needy. This is not permissible, and he will not be rewarded for this.

9

Mistakes Related to Fasting

1. Verbally stating the intention to fast.

It has been previously mentioned that verbalizing the intention is an action which was not done by the Prophet ﷺ, nor his Companions, nor the generation who came after the Companions, nor any of the four Imāms, nor any of the Salaf. Therefore, it is a newly invented matter and an innovation. The place of the intention is the heart. It is the intent of the worship. There are authentic narrations in which the Prophet ﷺ made it a condition that the person must have the intention to fast before Fajr, in the case of obligatory fasting. It has been narrated from the Mother of the Believers, Hafsah رضي الله عنها that the Prophet ﷺ said:

مَنْ لَمْ يُبَيِّتِ اَلصِّيَامَ قَبْلَ اَلْفَجْرِ فَلَا صِيَامَ لَهُ.

"Whoever does not plan to fast before Fajr, there is no fast for him."[1]

Meaning, he has the intention in his heart to fast. And this is apparent from the meaning of the word "plan" (بَيَّتَ). And Allāh knows best.

[1] *Jāmi' at-Tirmidhī* 730

2. Being careless regarding the time to stop eating before fasting.

Some of the people eat and drink until the caller to prayer has completed the *adhān*. And perhaps they are so careless that they continue to eat and drink until all the callers to prayer in the various *masājid* complete the *adhān* which they can hear. This is an obvious error and perhaps it invalidates the fast. Allāh the Exalted said:

$$ \{ \text{وَكُلُوا وَاشْرَبُوا حَتَّى يَتَبَيَّنَ لَكُمُ الْخَيْطُ الْأَبْيَضُ مِنَ الْخَيْطِ الْأَسْوَدِ مِنَ الْفَجْرِ} \} $$

Eat and drink until the white thread (light) of dawn appears to you distinct from the black thread (darkness of night).

[Sūrah al-Baqarah 2:187]

The time mentioned in the verse—when the dawn becomes clear—is at the first entrance of Fajr, at the time the *adhān* for Fajr is called. The word "until" denotes the purpose or intent. Thus, when the caller starts the second *adhān* after the entrance of Fajr, it is obligatory to refrain from everything which invalidates the fast, and the person must begin fasting at this point. This is the meaning of the *ḥadīth* narrated by 'Ā'ishah and Ibn 'Umar ؓ. The Prophet ﷺ said:

$$ \text{إِنَّ بِلَالًا يُؤَذِّنُ بِلَيْلٍ فَكُلُوا وَاشْرَبُوا حَتَّى يُؤَذِّنَ ابْنُ أُمِّ مَكْتُومٍ.} $$

"Bilāl calls the *adhān* at night, so eat and drink until you hear the *adhān* of Ibn Umm Maktūm, for he does not call the *adhān* until Fajr enters."[2]

The statement of the Prophet ﷺ: "eat and drink until…" is evidence for the obligation to stop eating and begin fasting upon hearing the second *adhān* which is called after Fajr enters.

---

[2] *Ṣaḥīḥ Muslim* 1092

There are *aḥādīth* narrated which give an allowance for the person who hears the *adhān* when he has food or drink in his hand to take what he needs from it. And Allāh knows best.

---

3. Being careless concerning praying in congregation, sleeping through the prayer, and joining all the prayers together.

This is from the great evils during the month of Ramaḍān, as prayer is the greatest pillar of Islām after the two testimonies of faith. It is never permissible to be careless concerning the prayer. The obligation to pray in congregation in the *masjid* has already been mentioned in the section concerning the prayer. It is not permissible to be careless regarding the prayer by not praying in the *masjid* due to sleep, and combining the prayer without a legislative reason to combine is another sin and likewise not permissible.

The Muslim is commanded to organize his time by placing the prayer before every other matter. And it is upon the Muslim to assist one another in this matter, and to advise one another concerning this issue, which is seen throughout the month of Ramaḍān. Allāh the Exalted said:

﴿ وَتَعَاوَنُوا عَلَى الْبِرِّ وَالتَّقْوَىٰ ۖ وَلَا تَعَاوَنُوا عَلَى الْإِثْمِ وَالْعُدْوَانِ ﴾

Help one another in righteousness and piety, but do not help one another in sin and transgression.

[Sūrah al-Mā'idah 5:2]

---

4. Engaging in false speech and acting upon it, and ignorance while fasting.

False speech and acting upon it is sin and not permissible, based upon what has been authenticated from Abū Hurayrah رضي الله عنه. He said that the

Prophet ﷺ said:

مَنْ لَمْ يَدَعْ قَوْلَ الزُّورِ وَالْعَمَلَ بِهِ فَلَيْسَ لِلَّهِ حَاجَةٌ فِي أَنْ يَدَعَ طَعَامَهُ وَشَرَابَهُ.

"Whoever does not give up false speech and acting upon it, Allāh has no need of his giving up his food and drink."[3]

Ignorance is by using foul language and insulting the people. This is bad etiquette, especially while fasting. The Prophet ﷺ said:

قَالَ اللَّهُ كُلُّ عَمَلِ ابْنِ آدَمَ لَهُ إِلاَّ الصِّيَامَ، فَإِنَّهُ لِي، وَأَنَا أَجْزِي بِهِ. وَالصِّيَامُ جُنَّةٌ، وَإِذَا كَانَ يَوْمُ صَوْمِ أَحَدِكُمْ، فَلاَ يَرْفُثْ وَلاَ يَصْخَبْ، فَإِنْ سَابَّهُ أَحَدٌ، أَوْ قَاتَلَهُ فَلْيَقُلْ إِنِّي امْرُؤٌ صَائِمٌ.

"Allāh said, 'All the deeds of the son of Ādam are for them, except fasting, for surely that is for Me, and I will give the reward for it.' Fasting is a shield, and when one of you is fasting, let him not commit any obscenity or quarrel. If somebody should quarrel with him, he should say, 'I am fasting.'"[4]

The Prophet ﷺ said:

لَيْسَ الصِّيَامُ مِنَ الأَكْلِ وَالشُّرْبِ، إِنَّمَا الصِّيَامُ مِنَ اللَّغْوِ وَالرَّفَثِ، فَإِنْ سَابَّكَ أَحَدٌ أَوْ جَهِلَ عَلَيْكَ، فَلْتَقُلْ: إِنِّي صَائِمٌ، إِنِّي صَائِمٌ.

"Fasting does not just mean abstaining from food and drink; rather, fasting means abstaining from idle and obscene speech. If someone insults you or treats you in an ignorant manner, then say, 'I am fasting, I am fasting.'"[5]

---

[3] *Ṣaḥīḥ al-Bukhārī* 1804

[4] *Ṣaḥīḥ al-Bukhārī* 1771

[5] Narrated by Ibn Khuzaymah (1879).

The first *ḥadīth* mentioned from Abū Hurayrah has a different wording:

مَنْ لَمْ يَدَعْ قَوْلَ الزُّورِ وَالْعَمَلَ بِهِ وَالْجَهْلَ...

"Whoever does not give up false speech and acting upon it and ignorance..."[6]

Ignorance includes all indecent speech, insults, backbiting, tale carrying, lying, false speech, and all the ills of the tongue and limbs.

Thus, it is obligatory upon the fasting person to remove himself from lying, backbiting, and insults. This is also obligatory upon the person who is not fasting, but the prohibition is greater for the fasting person. And Allāh is the One Who grants success in abandoning these ills.

---

5. Looking at and listening to the impermissible.

Allāh the Exalted said:

﴿ إِنَّ السَّمْعَ وَالْبَصَرَ وَالْفُؤَادَ كُلُّ أُولَـٰئِكَ كَانَ عَنْهُ مَسْئُولًا ﴾

Verily! The hearing, the sight, and the heart of each of you will be questioned.

[Sūrah al-Isrā' 17:36]

The people shall be questioned about how they utilized the limbs they have been entrusted with. Some people are accustomed to looking at and listening to evil, such as looking at naked women who call to lewdness, or listening to music and the like. It is obligatory to abandon this during Ramaḍān and outside of Ramaḍān, although abandoning this during Ramaḍān is greater due to this pure month, its sanctity, and the status of the month of obedience and forgiveness. How wonderful is it for the Muslim to use this month as an opportu-

[6] *Ṣaḥīḥ al-Bukhārī* 6057

nity to break his ties to these impermissible vices of the eye and ear, as well as the other desires! It is stated in the narration:

يَدَعُ طَعَامَهُ وَشَرَابَهُ وَشَهْوَتَهُ مِنْ أَجْلِي.

"He leaves his food, drink, and desires for My sake."[7]

---

6. Listening to music during the month of Ramaḍān and outside of Ramaḍān.

There is proof from the Book and the Sunnah that listening to musical instruments and the like is not permissible. Allāh the Exalted said:

﴿ وَمِنَ النَّاسِ مَن يَشْتَرِي لَهْوَ الْحَدِيثِ لِيُضِلَّ عَن سَبِيلِ اللَّهِ ﴾

And of mankind is he who purchases idle talk to mislead (men) from the path of Allāh.

[Sūrah Luqmān 31:6]

Ibn Mas'ūd ﷺ and others have said: "Idle talk" means singing, and there is no doubt that musical instruments and music is included in idle talk which leads the people away from the path of Allāh.

In *Ṣaḥīḥ al-Bukhārī,* there is a narration which some of the scholars mention connects various acts that are impermissible:

لَيَكُونَنَّ مِنْ أُمَّتِي أَقْوَامٌ يَسْتَحِلُّونَ الْحِرَ وَالْحَرِيرَ وَالْخَمْرَ وَالْمَعَازِفَ.

"Among my nation, there will certainly be people who permit fornication, silk, alcohol, and musical instruments…"[8]

This clearly shows its prohibition, because something is only permit-

---

[7] *Al-Bukhārī* and *Muslim*

[8] *Ṣaḥīḥ al-Bukhārī* 5590

ted if it was unlawful. And the Prophet ﷺ spoke the truth, for surely there are some people from the *ummah* of Muḥammad who use musical instruments and singing as though they are permissible, and they do not view them as impermissible. It is obligatory upon the Muslim to follow that which comes in the Qur'ān and the Sunnah and to abandon the impermissible acts during the month of fasting—as the prohibition is stronger during this time—and outside the month of fasting.

---

7. Being careless with learning the rules and regulations of fasting.

It is obligatory upon the Muslim to know the clear rules and regulations of fasting which are binding upon him, such as the time to begin fasting and the time to complete the fast, what invalidates the fast, what he is prohibited from, the conditions of the fast, and the like. This is in order for his worship to be in its proper place and so he will be rewarded for it, due to the virtue of this knowledge.

10

Mistakes Related to Ḥajj

---

1. Believing it is obligatory to pray two *raka'āt* upon entering *iḥrām*.[1]

There is no proof that this is obligatory; rather, the Prophet ﷺ used to don the garment of *iḥrām* after praying an obligatory prayer, so it is the Sunnah to don *iḥrām* after an obligatory prayer. Some of the scholars have said that it is recommended to pray two *raka'āt* of *iḥrām* before entering *iḥrām* for the pilgrimage. This is based upon the authentic narration in which Jibrīl said to the Prophet ﷺ:

صَلِّ فِي هَذَا الْوَادِي الْمُبَارَكِ وَقُلْ عُمْرَةٌ وَحَجَّةٌ.

"Pray in this blessed valley and say, ''Umrah along with Ḥajj.'"[2]

This proves that it is recommended to pray an optional prayer before *iḥrām*.

---

[1] **Translator's note:** *Iḥrām* is a state of ritual consecration observed during Ḥajj and 'Umrah. During this time, the male pilgrim dons the garments of *iḥrām*.

[2] *Ṣaḥīḥ al-Bukhārī* 1534

2. Apathy towards engaging in the prohibitions while in a state of *iḥrām*.

This is the same as apathy towards the obligations of Ḥajj. Thus, it is obligatory to learn the various prohibitions during the state of *iḥrām*. These are the things the person must avoid while in a state of *iḥrām*. Allāh the Exalted said:

﴿وَلَا تَحْلِقُوا رُءُوسَكُمْ حَتَّىٰ يَبْلُغَ الْهَدْيُ مَحِلَّهُ﴾

And do not shave your heads until the sacrificial animal reaches the place of sacrifice

[Sūrah al-Baqarah 2:196]

The Prophet ﷺ said:

لَا يَلْبَسُ الْمُحْرِمُ الْقَمِيصَ وَلَا السَّرَاوِيلَ وَلَا الْبُرْنُسَ وَلَا الْخُفَّيْنِ إِلَّا أَنْ لَا يَجِدَ النَّعْلَيْنِ فَلْيَلْبَسْ مَا هُوَ أَسْفَلُ مِنَ الْكَعْبَيْنِ وَلَا ثَوْباً مَسَّهُ زَعْفَرَانٌ وَلَا وَرْسٌ.

"The *muḥrim* (person in a state of *iḥrām*) should not wear shirts, trousers, a hooded garment, or leather socks, except for one who cannot find sandals, in which case he may wear leather socks but he should cut them (so that they are) lower than the ankles. And do not wear any clothes that have been dyed with saffron or *warss*[3]."[4]

These are some of the prohibitions, and it is obligatory to learn the remaining prohibitions and avoid them in order to safeguard the Ḥajj and receive the complete reward for it.

---

3. The woman not covering properly in front of unrelated men.

[3] **Translator's note:** *Warss* is a plant that produces a yellow dye.

[4] *Ṣaḥīḥ al-Bukhārī* 5458; *Ṣaḥīḥ Muslim* (1177)

It is obligatory upon the woman to cover her face and her entire body in the presence of non-related, marriageable men during Ḥajj and outside of Ḥajj. But during Ḥajj, if the woman is not in the presence of non-related men, then she uncovers her face, as has been authenticated by 'Ā'ishah ﵂. She said:

كَانَ الرُّكْبَانُ يَمُرُّونَ بِنَا وَنَحْنُ مَعَ رَسُولِ اللَّهِ صَلَّى اللَّهُ عَلَيْهِ وَسَلَّمَ مُحْرِمَاتٌ، فَإِذَا حَاذَوْا بِنَا سَدَلَتْ إِحْدَانَا جِلْبَابَهَا مِنْ رَأْسِهَا عَلَى وَجْهِهَا، فَإِذَا جَاوَزُونَا كَشَفْنَاهُ.

"Riders would pass us when we accompanied the Messenger of Allāh ﷺ while we were in the state of *iḥrām*. When they came by us, one of us would let down her outer garment from her head over her face, and when they had passed on, we would uncover our faces."[5]

---

4. Women wearing clothes which resemble the men's clothing.

This is prohibited. The women are commanded by the legislation of Islām to avoid resembling men in their dress and appearance. Some women wear clothes that resemble men's clothing or robes resembling men's robes. Women don't have any specific garments for *iḥrām,* while she is categorically prohibited from imitating men. Ibn 'Abbās ﵄ said:

لَعَنَ رَسُولُ اللَّهِ صَلَّى اللهُ عَلَيْهِ وَسَلَّمَ الْمُتَشَبِّهِينَ مِنَ الرِّجَالِ بِالنِّسَاءِ، وَالْمُتَشَبِّهَاتِ مِنَ النِّسَاءِ بِالرِّجَالِ.

"The Messenger of Allāh ﷺ cursed men who imitate women and women who imitate men."[6]

Al-Ḥafiẓ (Ibn Ḥajar) mentioned in his explanation of *Ṣaḥīḥ*

---

[5] *Sunan Abī Dāwūd* 1833; *ḥadīth hasan.*

[6] *Ṣaḥīḥ al-Bukhārī* 5885

al-Bukhārī: "Some of the scholars have said that what is meant by the prohibited resembling is resembling men in their garb, some manly characteristics, movements, and the like; not meaning resembling men in the affairs of good."

---

5. Taking photographs during the rites of Ḥajj, such as pictures for mementos.

The evidence has proven that pictures of all types are not permissible. The evidence for the prohibition of pictures is general and it does not specify a certain type of picture.

Ibn Mas'ūd ﷺ said, "I heard the Messenger of Allāh ﷺ saying:

إِنَّ أَشَدَّ النَّاسِ عَذَابًا يَوْمَ الْقِيَامَةِ الْمُصَوِّرُونَ.

"'Verily, the most severely punished people of the Day of Judgment will be the picture makers.'"[7]

In the Arabic language, the word "picture maker" (الْمُصَوِّرُونَ) is known as an agent noun[8] (اسم فاعل), and the definite article is attached to it; thus, this format in the Arabic language shows that it is general to include all types of pictures, and there is not a permissible type of picture except for pictures of objects that do not contain souls. The evidence proves that taking pictures of objects without souls is permissible. The word "pictures" includes photographs, based upon the language and custom; thus, it is included in the prohibition. The prohibition of picture making includes the means that facilitate picture making. And that which is prohibited in order to block a path to harm is allowed when there is a prevailing benefit. For this reason, pictures for identification cards, licenses, and the like are allowed due

---

[7] *Ṣaḥīḥ Muslim* 2109

[8] **Translator's note:** An agent noun is a word that is derived from another word denoting an action, which identifies an entity that does that action. For example, "driver" is an agent noun formed from the verb "drive." (Panther, Klaus-Uwe; Thornburg, Linda L.; Barcelona, Antonio (2009). *Metonymy and Metaphor in Grammar*)

to the benefit and there being no alternative, although it is hated and not advised. And Allāh knows best.

---

6. Kissing or rubbing the walls or doors of the Ka'bah.

All of these actions are innovations and newly invented matters. As for rubbing the stones and various doors of the Ka'bah, seeking blessings from the stones and walls, this is *shirk*. This is because seeking blessings is to seek benefit and good, and this cannot be sought from stones and wood. This was mentioned in the section of *'aqīdah* in the *ḥadīth* of Dhāt Anwāt. And the proof and evidence for this matter is clear.

As for the walls of the Ka'bah, it is not legislated to rub them. It is only legislated to kiss and rub the black stone, and to touch the Yemeni corner. And it has been affirmed in the Sunnah that the person may place his chest, cheek, forearm, and body at the *multazam* (place of clinging)[9]. This has been narrated; it is the Sunnah and it is prescribed to do so, as it was done by the Prophet ﷺ. As for the other walls of the Ka'bah, its pillars, and its curtain, wiping them or kissing them is an innovation.

How wonderful is the retraction of Mu'āwiyah from wiping the two corners of the Ka'bah on the side of Shām, and accepting the statement of Ibn 'Abbās. Mu'āwiyah ﷺ said, "There is no spot on the Sacred House which is to be abandoned." Ibn 'Abbās ﷺ said:

﴿ لَّقَدْ كَانَ لَكُمْ فِي رَسُولِ اللَّهِ أُسْوَةٌ حَسَنَةٌ ﴾

Indeed, in the Messenger of Allāh you have an excellent example.

[Sūrah al-Aḥzāb 33:21]

---

[9] The *multazam* is the part of the Ka'bah that is between the Black Stone and the door of the Ka'bah.

Muʿāwiyah said, "You have spoken the truth."[10]

In similar fashion, it is upon the Muslim to return to the affirmed Sunnah and abandon innovation and newly invented matters.

---

7. Facing Mount 'Arafah while supplicating with *du'ā'*, and climbing Mount 'Arafah as an act of worship.

Mount ʿArafah is not specified with a particular virtue. The Messenger of Allāh stood behind it, placing it in front of him in the direction of the *qiblah,* and said:

وَقَفْتُ هَا هُنَا وَعَرَفَةُ كُلُّهَا مَوْقِفٌ.

"I am standing here, but all of ʿArafah is the place of standing."[11]

Therefore, facing it while making *duʿā'* on the Day of ʿArafah or other days has no special virtue, nor is it a reason for the supplication being accepted; rather, if the person adheres to this practice and believes that it is more virtuous, this action becomes an innovation.

Climbing Mount ʿArafah as an act of worship and drawing near to Allāh is an innovation which was not done by the Prophet ﷺ. The Prophet ﷺ did not climb this Mount; rather, he only stood behind it. Thus climbing it as an act of worship—as it has been witnessed with the people crowding upon it—is an innovation and newly invented matter. And every innovation is misguidance. May Allāh enlighten the insight of the Muslims.

---

8. Visiting some of the monuments which are not prescribed to visit as an act of worship, such as visiting the cave of Hirā'.

All of this is innovation and newly invented matters. The Messenger

[10] Collected by Aḥmad and others.

[11] *Sunan Abī Dāwūd* 1907

of Allāh ﷺ did not go to any of these monuments, nor did his Companions or any of those who followed the Companions. And they preceded us to good and were more virtuous than those that followed them.

Exalting monuments by visiting them is a means to *shirk*. For this reason, 'Umar bin al-Khattab ﷺ saw people praying in a place they said the Prophet ﷺ used to pray in, he said:

إِنَّمَا أَهْلَكَ مَنْ كَانَ قَبْلَكُمْ بِأَشْبَاهِ هَذِهِ، يَتَّبِعُونَ آثَارَ أَنْبِيَائِهِمْ.

"Verily, those who came before you were only destroy by the like of this; following the remnants of their prophets."[12]

---

9. Believing that wearing white during *iḥrām* is better for women.

This is a mistake of the common people. The woman is not prohibited from wearing her garments during *iḥrām* with the exception of gloves and *niqab*. With the exception of these two, her clothes are permitted and there is not a particular type clothing which is better than another type of clothing.

The clothes of the woman should not display her beauty, the beauty of her body, the shape of her body, or show her forearms or shins. Ibn 'Umar ﷺ said about the Prophet ﷺ:

نَهَى النِّسَاءَ فِي إِحْرَامِهِنَّ عَنِ الْقُفَّازَيْنِ وَالنِّقَابِ وَمَا مَسَّ الْوَرْسُ وَالزَّعْفَرَانُ مِنَ الثِّيَابِ.

"He forbade women in the sacred state of *iḥrām* to wear gloves, face

---

[12] Collected by Sa'eed bin Mansour and Ibn Abī Shaybah with an authentic chain of narration.

veils and to wear clothes with dye of *warss*[13] or saffron on them.[14]

The women should not wear clothes stained with dye or clothes with adornments. When ʿAlī ؓ entered upon Fatimah, he found she had adorned a dyed garment and placed kohl on her eyes. He disapproved of this because he was not aware that she had exited from the state of *iḥrām* at the command of the Prophet ﷺ.

وَقَدِمَ عَلِيٌّ رضى الله عنه مِنَ الْيَمَنِ بِهَدْيٍ وَسَاقَ رَسُولُ اللَّهِ صلى الله عليه وسلم مِنَ الْمَدِينَةِ هَدْيًا وَإِذَا فَاطِمَةُ قَدْ لَبِسَتْ ثِيَابًا صَبِيغًا وَاكْتَحَلَتْ. قَالَ فَانْطَلَقْتُ مُحَرِّشًا أَسْتَفْتِي رَسُولَ اللَّهِ صلى الله عليه وسلم فَقُلْتُ يَا رَسُولَ اللَّهِ إِنَّ فَاطِمَةَ لَبِسَتْ ثِيَابًا صَبِيغًا وَاكْتَحَلَتْ وَقَالَتْ أَمَرَنِي بِهِ أَبِي صلى الله عليه وسلم. قَالَ صَدَقَتْ صَدَقَتْ صَدَقَتْ أَنَا أَمَرْتُهَا.

ʿAlī ؓ came from Yemen with an animal for sacrifice, while the Messenger of Allāh ﷺ brought an animal for sacrifice from al-Madinah. Fatimah had put on a dyed garment and applied kohl to her eyes, and he (ʿAlī) said, "I went to the Prophet to complain about that and to ask whether she could do that. I said, 'O Messenger of Allāh, Fatima had put on a dyed garment and applied kohl to her eyes, and she said, "My father ﷺ told me to do that."' He said, 'She is telling the truth, she is telling the truth, she is telling the truth; I told her to do that.'"[15]

Thus it was as though it was affirmed amongst them that the woman is prohibited from wearing dyed clothes with adornments (during the state of *iḥrām*) but after that she can wear any color clothing she likes, and various types of silk, and garments and long as it completely covers her body from non-related men.

---

[13] **Translator's note:** *Warss* is a plant that produces a yellow dye

[14] *Sunan Abī Dāwūd* 1827

[15] *Sunan an-Nasā'ī* 2712

10. Believing Ḥajj is not complete without visiting the grave of the Prophet ﷺ.

This belief is widespread amongst the common people in some countries, and it is outright error, because the pillars of Ḥajj, its obligations, and its *sunan* do not include visiting the grave. This fact has been agreed upon by the Companions, those that followed them, and the well-known Imāms of this religion from the early virtuous generations, and by the four Imāms. None of the narrations which mention visiting the grave of the Prophet ﷺ after Ḥajj are authentic. If the pilgrim desires to pray in the *masjid* of the Prophet ﷺ, this is a recommended action, and the virtue of the prayer being multiplied one thousand times[16].

Therefore, if the intention is to pray in the Prophet's *masjid*; this is recommended due to its virtue. When he enters the *masjid* he prays what has been decreed for him to pray and then he conveys the *salām* to the Prophet ﷺ. And those who are in near proximity to him and those who are far from him are the same in regard to conveying the *salām* and the return of the *salām*. He should not utter any falsehood[17], and he should not stand there for a long time; rather he should only give the *salām* and then move on. This is what is beloved to the Prophet ﷺ.

11. Believing the authenticity of some fabricated *aḥādīth.*

From these fabricated *ḥadīth* are the following:

[16] **Translator's note:** The Prophet ﷺ said, "One prayer in this *masjid* of mine is better than one thousand prayers offered anywhere else, except al-Masjid al-Haram." Narrated by al-Bukhārī (1190); *Ṣaḥīḥ Muslim* 1394.

[17] **Translator's note:** The Messenger of Allāh be upon him said, "I used to forbid you to visit graves, but now whoever wants to visit them let him do so, but do not utter any falsehood." Narrated by an-Nasā'ī (2033); classed as *ṣaḥīḥ* by al-Albāni in *As-Silsilah as-Sahihah* (886).

من حج البيت ولم يزرني فقد جفاني.

"Whoever performs Ḥajj to the Sacred House and does not visit me, has shunned me."[18]

من زار قبري وقبر أبي ابراهيم في عام فقد وجبت له الشفاعة.

"Whoever visits my grave and the grave of my father Ibrāhīm during the year, the intercession has surely become mandatory for him."

إذا ضاقت الأمور فعليكم بأصحاب القبور.

"If your affairs become difficult, go to the inhabitants of the graves."[19]

لو اعتقد أحدكم في حجر لنفعه.

"If one of you believed in a stone, it would benefit him."[20]

These narrations are lies; the scholars have stated these narrations are fabrications with no basis.

---

12. Walking backwards after the farewell *ṭawāf.*

This is an innovation and newly invented matter. It has not been narrated that the Prophet ﷺ or his Companions did this after performing the farewell *ṭawāf*, thus it is a newly invented matter and believing it to be correct is an innovation.

---

13. Performing *ṭawāf* around the grave of the Prophet ﷺ.

[18] **Translator's note:** *Tarteeb al-Mawdoo'āt* by adh-Dhahabi (600); *Al-Mawdoo'āt* by as-Saghāni (52); *Al-Fawā'id al-Majmoo'ah* by ash-Shawkāni (326).

[19] **Translator's note:** Shaykh 'Uthaymeen said this is not a *ḥadīth* from the Prophet ﷺ. This is major *shirk*, as it directs people to go and pray to the inhabitants of the graves.

[20] **Translator's note:** Shaykh Al Albāni said, "Ibn Taymiyyah said this is a fabrication."

This is *shirk*; and with Allāh refuge is sought. *Tawāf* is worship. Those who perform *tawāf* around the grave of the Prophet ﷺ have made his grave into an idol. The Prophet ﷺ said:

اللَّهُمَّ لاَ تَجْعَلْ قَبْرِي وَثَنًا يُعْبَدُ.

"O Allāh, do not make my grave an idol that is worshiped."[21]

Allāh the Exalted protected his grave and answered his supplication, thus his grave is not accessible. Thus the people have made his room and his house like the house of Allāh and thus the perform *tawāf* around it. This is *shirk*. The only house which *tawāf* is performed around is the house of Allāh (the Ka'bah), which has been prescribed for *tawāf*.

---

14. Apathy towards spending the night at Muzdalifah and Mina.

Spending the night of sacrifice at Muzdalifah and staying overnight in Mina during the Days of Tashrīq is from the obligations of Ḥajj. Allāh the Exalted said:

﴿ فَإِذَا أَفَضْتُم مِّنْ عَرَفَاتٍ فَاذْكُرُوا اللَّهَ عِندَ الْمَشْعَرِ الْحَرَامِ ﴾

Then when you leave 'Arafah, remember Allāh at the sites of the Ḥaram.

[Sūrah al-Baqarah 2:198]

This is proof of its obligation, because the Messenger of Allāh ﷺ explained this command with his action in obedience to Allāh. He remained in Muzdalifah until he prayed Fajr prayer there and it became very light outside. But he gave an allowance for those who were weak to leave Muzdalifah after half the night. 'Ā'ishah رضي الله عنها said:

---

[21] *Muwatta Malik*

أَنَّ سَوْدَةَ، كَانَتِ امْرَأَةً ثَبِطَةً فَاسْتَأْذَنَتْ رَسُولَ اللَّهِ - صلى الله عليه وسلم - أَنْ تَدْفَعَ مِنْ جَمْعٍ قَبْلَ دُفْعَةِ النَّاسِ فَأَذِنَ لَهَا.

"Sawdah was a slow-moving woman, so she asked the Messenger of Allāh ﷺ for permission to depart from the night of Muzdalifah ahead of the people, and he gave her permission."[22]

Ibn 'Abbās رضي الله عنه said:

كُنْتُ فِيمَنْ قَدَّمَ النَّبِيُّ صلى الله عليه وسلم لَيْلَةَ الْمُزْدَلِفَةِ فِي ضَعَفَةِ أَهْلِهِ.

"I was one those whom the Prophet ﷺ sent ahead on the night of Muzdalifah among the weak ones of his family."[23]

Asma' رضي الله عنها said:

إِنَّ النَّبِيَّ صلى الله عليه وسلم أَذِنَ لِلظُّعُنِ.

"The Prophet ﷺ granted permission to the women."[24]

This includes the women who had an excuse and those who did not. The pilgrim has obeyed the command and performed the obligation of spending the night at Muzdalifah if they stay most of the night, and that means more than half or a little more than that. This is the viewpoint of most of the people of knowledge.

Likewise, staying at Mina during its nights is an obligation. An allowance is made for those who have an excuse to spend the night in Makkah or other places; such as those individuals who give water to the pilgrims or take care of their needs. This is proven by the *ḥadīth* of Ibn 'Abbās رضي الله عنه. He said:

---

22 *Ṣaḥīḥ Muslim* 1290

23 *Sunan an-Nasā'ī* 3033

24 *Ṣaḥīḥ Muslim* 1291

اسْتَأْذَنَ الْعَبَّاسُ رَسُولَ اللَّهِ صلى الله عليه وسلم - أَنْ يَبِيتَ بِمَكَّةَ أَيَّامَ مِنًى مِنْ أَجْلِ سِقَايَتِهِ فَأَذِنَ لَهُ.

"'Abbās asked the Messenger of Allāh ﷺ for permission to stay overnight in Makkah on the nights of Mina for the purpose of supplying water to the pilgrims, and he gave him permission."[25]

That which is not obligatory can be done without seeking permission. Thus seeking permission is proof of its obligation. And this is contained in the statement of Allāh the Exalted:

﴿ وَاذْكُرُوا اللَّهَ فِي أَيَّامٍ مَّعْدُودَاتٍ ﴾

And remember Allāh during the appointed Days.

[Sūrah al-Baqarah 2:203]

Asim ﷺ said:

أَنَّ رَسُولَ اَللَّهِ - صلى الله عليه وسلم -أَرْخَصَ لِرُعَاةِ اَلْإِبِلِ فِي اَلْبَيْتُوتَةِ عَنْ مِنًى.

"The Messenger of Allāh ﷺ excused the herdsmen of camels from sleeping at Mina."[26]

This excuse given to the herdsmen proves that without an excuse it remains an obligation.

---

15. Staying up at night for a long time without a need to do so.

This is in opposition to the Sunnah. As comes in the *ḥadīth* of Ja'far bin Muḥammad ﷺ. He said:

---

[25] *Sunan Abī Dāwūd* 1959

[26] *Bulugh al-Maram* 771

أَتَى الْمُزْدَلِفَةَ فَصَلَّى بِهَا الْمَغْرِبَ وَالْعِشَاءَ بِأَذَانٍ وَاحِدٍ وَإِقَامَتَيْنِ وَلَمْ يُسَبِّحْ بَيْنَهُمَا شَيْئًا ثُمَّ اضْطَجَعَ حَتَّى طَلَعَ الْفَجْرُ.

"He came to Muzdalifah and he prayed Maghrib and 'Ishā' with one *adhān* and two *iqāmah* with no glorification in between, then he laid down until Fajr entered."[27]

Therefore, it is from the guidance of the Prophet ﷺ to avoid staying up after 'Ishā' except if there is a need such as knowledge or a benefit.

---

16. The belief that wearing a watch or sandals with thread is prohibited.

This is a mistake. The person is a state of *iḥrām* is prohibited from wearing sewn clothing. And the meaning of sewn clothing is the garments stitched according to the limbs of the body like a Thoub or pants and the like. The word 'sewn garments' was mentioned by some of the Salaf explaining the statement of the Prophet ﷺ:

لَا يَلْبَسُ الْمُحْرِمُ الْقَمِيصَ وَلَا السَّرَاوِيلَ وَلَا الْبُرْنُسَ وَلَا الْخُفَّيْنِ إِلَّا أَنْ لَا يَجِدَ النَّعْلَيْنِ فَلْيَلْبَسْ مَا هُوَ أَسْفَلُ مِنْ الْكَعْبَيْنِ وَلاَ ثَوْباً مَسَّهُ زَعْفَرانٌ وَلاَ وَرْسٌ.

"The *muḥrim* (person in a state of *iḥrām*) should not wear shirts, trousers, a hooded garment, or leather socks, except for one who cannot find sandals, in which case he may wear leather socks but he should cut them (so that they are) lower than the ankles. And do not wear any clothes that have been dyed with saffron or *warss*."[28]

Thus it is permissible for the person in a state of *iḥrām* to wear sandals as they are. As for watches and the like, the person can avoid wearing

---

[27] *Sunan Ibn Mājah*

[28] *Al-Bukhārī* (5458) and *Muslim* (1177)

them to be on the safe side, based upon the statement of Ibn 'Umar رضي الله عنهما:

لا تعقد عليك شيئا.

"Do not attach to yourselves anything."[29]

And Allāh knows best.

---

17. Using musical instruments during Ḥajj and outside of Ḥajj.

It is not permissible to utilize musicians or musical instruments. The proof for this was mentioned in the section on fasting.

---

18. Stoning the *jamarāt* before the appropriate time.

If the person stones the *jamarāt* before the appropriate time it does not count and they must return to stone at the appropriate time. The time for stoning the *jamarāt* is on the day of sacrifice (Eid) for the entire day, or during the night of Eid (at the end of the night) for those who left Muzdalifah at the end of the night. Also this can be done during the days at Mina after the sun has passed its zenith. This has been affirmed in *Ṣaḥīḥ al-Bukhārī* from the *ḥadīth* of Ibn 'Umar, he said:

كُنَّا نَتَحَيَّنُ فَإِذَا زَالَتِ الشَّمْسُ رَمَيْنَا.

"We used to wait until the sun passed its meridian, then we stoned (the *jamarāt*)."[30]

Jābir رضي الله عنه said:

رأيت رسول الله صلى الله عليه وسلم يرمي الجمرة ضحى يوم النحر،

[29] Collected by Ibn Abī Shaybah in *The Book of Hajj*.

[30] *Ṣaḥīḥ al-Bukhārī* 1746

ورمى بعد ذلك بعد زوال الشمس.

"I saw the Messenger of Allāh ﷺ stoning the *jamarāt* at the forenoon on the day of sacrifice, and after that he stoned it after the sun had passed the meridian."[31]

---

19. Washing the stones before throwing them.

This is a mistake because the stones are not impure. And it is not a condition that they be pure. The Messenger of Allāh ﷺ throw the stones without washing them, and in the Messenger of Allāh ﷺ we have an excellent example.

Al-Muwaffaq رحمه الله said: "It has been narrated from Aḥmad that this (washing the stones) is not recommended and it has not reached us that this was done by the Prophet ﷺ. And this position is correct. It is likewise the position of 'Ata, Malik, and many of the scholars. The Prophet ﷺ collected stones as he rode upon his camel. He held them in his hand and he did not wash them nor did he order anyone to wash them. Washing the stones has no required significance. If the person throws stones which are impure, it suffices because it is a pebble."

---

20. Women crowding with the men at the Black Stone.

The woman is an *'awrah* and it is upon her to avoid crowding with the men. She must go towards that which will cause her to fall into sin and decrease her Ḥajj or her obligations by crowding with the men or being a sight for them to look at.

Kissing the black stone is not obligatory. For those who are able to do so with ease without crowding, then this is good; if not, it is obligatory to avoid crowding. The Prophet ﷺ said to 'Umar:

---

[31] *Ṣaḥīḥ Muslim* 1299

يا عمر إنك رجل قوي لا تزاحم على الحجر.

"O 'Umar, you are a strong man; do not crowd around the stone."[32]

This has been collected by Aḥmad with some weakness in the chain of narration.

Crowding which entails that which is forbidden in the legislation is prohibited. It has been collected in *Ṣaḥīḥ al-Bukhārī*:

كَانَتْ عَائِشَةُ رضى الله عنها تَطُوفُ حَجْرَةً مِنَ الرِّجَالِ لاَ تُخَالِطُهُمْ، فَقَالَتِ امْرَأَةٌ انْطَلِقِي نَسْتَلِمْ يَا أُمَّ الْمُؤْمِنِينَ. قَالَتْ انطَلِقِي عَنْكِ. وَأَبَتْ.

"'Ā'ishah ﵂ used to perform *tawāf* around the stone separately from the men and never mixed with them. Once a woman said to her, 'O Mother of the Believers, let's go touch the stone.' Ā'ishah responded:,'You go without me.' And she refused to go."[33]

This statement was disapproval from 'Ā'ishah ﵂.

---

21. Entrusting others to throw the stones on your behalf without necessity.

There is no problem with women and the weak entrusting others to throw the stones on their behalf, due to the crowding and harm that occurs. But if there is no crowding or harm, there is no excuse. A group of scholars said: Entrusting someone to throw the stones on another's behalf is permissible for supererogatory acts are allowed outright, for those who have the ability or those who do not have the ability.

---

[32] Classed as strong by al-Albāni in his treatise on the rites of Ḥajj and 'Umrah.

[33] *Ṣaḥīḥ al-Bukhārī* 1618

22. Believing the Shayṭān is present where the stones are thrown at the *jamarāt.*

This is incorrect. These three places are the places where Shaytān appeared to our Prophet Ibrāhīm ﷺ. Thus these are places of worship, where Allāh is worshiped by throwing the stones and remembering Him. Shaytān is not present standing upon the *jamarāt.*

23. Leaving 'Arafah before sunset, and leaving Muzdalifah before half of the night.

As for remaining in 'Arafah until after the sun has set; this is obligatory. The Prophet ﷺ remained there until the sun set and the yellow afterglow had diminished a little. This is the meaning of the *ḥadīth* of Jābir[34].

Therefore it is mandatory to remain in 'Arafah for a part of the night even if just for a small portion of it based upon the *ḥadīth* of Urwah bin Mudarris.[35]

Whoever departs before sunset must offer a sacrifice as atonement.

Likewise remaining and spending the night in Muzdalifah is obligatory. This was done by the Prophet ﷺ. He only gave an allowed to the weak amongst them and the women and those with them as previously mentioned. Whoever does not remain in Muzdalifah until half the night has abandoned an obligation. The Prophet ﷺ said:

خُذُوا عَنِّي مَنَاسِكَكُمْ.

---

[34] *Sunan Abī Dāwūd* 1905

[35] **Translator's note:** Urwah bin Mudarris said: "I saw the Messenger of Allāh standing in Muzdalifah and he said: 'Whoever offers this prayer with us here then stands with us and stood before that in 'Arafah by night or by day, his Hajj is complete. *Sunan an-Nasā'ī* 3039

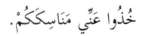

"Take from me your rituals [of Ḥajj]."[36]

---

24. Fasting the day of 'Arafah for those standing on 'Arafah.

The Prophet ﷺ did not fast the day of 'Arafah while present at 'Arafah. It was narrated by Maymunah ﵂:

إِنَّ النَّاسَ شَكُّوا فِي صِيَامِ رَسُولِ اللَّهِ صلى الله عليه وسلم يَوْمَ عَرَفَةَ فَأَرْسَلَتْ إِلَيْهِ مَيْمُونَةُ بِحِلاَبِ اللَّبَنِ وَهُوَ وَاقِفٌ فِي الْمَوْقِفِ فَشَرِبَ مِنْهُ وَالنَّاسُ يَنْظُرُونَ إِلَيْهِ.

"The people were not sure whether the Prophet ﷺ was fasting on the day of 'Arafah, so she sent him some milk when he was standing in 'Arafah, and he drank it while the people were looking towards him."[37]

---

25. Busying the people with collecting stones for the *jamarāt* when they first enter Muzdalifah.

It is from the guidance of the noble Prophet ﷺ that he collected stones the morning of the sacrifice. Ibn 'Abbās ﵄ said:

قال لي رسول الله صلى الله عليه وسلم غداة العقبة وهو واقف على راحلته: هات الْقُطْ لي قال: فلقطت له حصيات هن حصى الخذف، فوضعهن في يده، وقال: بأمثال هؤلاء فارموا ... وإياكم والغلو فإنما هلك من كان قبلكم بالغلو في الدين.

"The Messenger of Allāh ﷺ said to me on the morning of al-Aqabah when he was standing atop his camel: 'Come and pick up pebbles for me.' So I picked up for him pebbles which were a little bigger than

---

[36] Narrated by Muslim (1297).

[37] *Ṣaḥīḥ Muslim* 1124

a chickpea. He put them in his hand and said, 'With pebbles like this stone (the *jamarāt*)... and beware of going to extremes, for those who came before you were destroyed because of going to extremes in religion.'"[38]

---

[38] *Ibn Mājah* 3029

11

Mistakes Related to Business Transactions

1. Selling what the person does not possess without authorization from the owner.

This is not permissible. Hakim bin Hizam ﷺ said:

أَتَيْتُ رَسُولَ اللَّهِ صَلَّى اللَّهُ عَلَيْهِ وَسَلَّمَ، فَقُلْتُ: يَأْتِينِي الرَّجُلُ يَسْأَلُنِي مِنَ الْبَيْعِ مَا لَيْسَ عِنْدِي، أَبْتَاعُ لَهُ مِنَ السُّوقِ ثُمَّ أَبِيعُهُ ؟ قَالَ: لَا تَبِعْ مَا لَيْسَ عِنْدَكَ.

"I came to the Messenger of Allāh ﷺ and said, 'A man may come to me wanting to buy something that I do not possess; should I buy it for him from the marketplace then sell it to him?' He said, 'Do not sell that which you do not possess.'"[1]

The scholars have said the meaning of "that which you do not possess"

[1] Narrated by at-Tirmidhī 1232; an-Nasā'ī 4613; Abū Dāwūd 3503, Ibn Mājah 2187, Aḥmad 14887. Classified as *ṣaḥīḥ* by al-Albāni in *Irwa' al-Ghaleel* 1292.

means that which you do not own. There is a similar *ḥadīth* from Amr bin Shuaib narrated from his father by way of his grandfather; he said, the Prophet ﷺ said:

لاَ يَحِلُّ سَلَفٌ وَبَيْعٌ وَلاَ شَرْطَانِ فِي بَيْعٍ وَلاَ رِبْحُ مَا لَمْ يُضْمَنْ وَلاَ بَيْعُ مَا لَيْسَ عِنْدَكَ.

"It is not lawful to lend and sell at the same time, nor two conditions in a sale, nor to profit from what is not possessed, nor to sell what one does not have."[2]

---

2. Selling an unknown product.

An example of this is someone selling something the buyer has not seen, or does not comprehend by way of a detailed description. The sale of an unknown commodity is invalid and impermissible. There are prohibitions for transactions involving selling various types of unknown commodities; such as selling the spoils of war before they have been distributed[3], and transactions known as *Mulamash* and *Munabadhaha*[4], and transactions known as *Hasah* (transactions determined by throwing a stone) and *Gharar* (transactions which involved some uncertainty)[5], and *Habal al-Habalah* (selling the offspring

[2] *Jāmi' at-Tirmidhī* 1234

[3] **Translator's note:** Narrated by Abū Hurayrah: The Messenger of Allāh ﷺ forbade selling spoils of war until they are distributed (*Sunan Abī Dāwūd* 3369).

[4] **Translator's note:** Abū Sa'eed Al-Khudri said: "The Messenger of Allāh ﷺ forbade two kinds of garments and two kinds of transactions. As for the two kinds of transactions, they are Mulamash and Munabadhaha. Munabadha is when a man says, 'I throw this garment, and the transaction becomes binding, and Mulamasah is when a man touches a garment with his hand, without spreading it out and checking it, and once he touches it, the transaction becomes binding." (*Sunan an-Nasā'ī* 4515).

[5] **Translator's note:** Abū Hurayrah said:"The Messenger of Allāh ﷺ prohibited the Gharar sale, and the Hasah sale." (*Jāmi' at-Tirmidhī* 1230) Imām Shafi'i said: "The Gharar sale includes selling fish that are in the water, selling a runaway slave, selling birds that are in the sky, and similar type of sales. And the meaning of Hasah sale is when the seller says to the buyer: 'When I toss the pebble at you, then the sale between you and I is final.'

of an unborn offspring)[6], and fish which are still in the water and similar transactions. There are affirmed prohibitions for all of these transactions in the Sunnah. This type of sell is prohibited due to the uncertainty it involves; either uncertainty of the specific production or its description. Selling an unknown product is prohibited and the prohibition necessitates that the transaction is invalid.

---

3. Selling a product without clarifying a known defect.

This is deception. The Prophet ﷺ said:

مَنْ غَشَّنَا فَلَيْسَ مِنَّا.

"Whoever deceives us is not from us."[7]

It is not permissible to conceal the defect of a product. Ubah bin Āmir ﷺ said, "I heard the Prophet ﷺ say:

الْمُسْلِمُ أَخُو الْمُسْلِمِ وَلاَ يَحِلُّ لِمُسْلِمٍ بَاعَ مِنْ أَخِيهِ بَيْعًا فِيهِ عَيْبٌ إِلاَّ بَيَّنَهُ لَهُ.

"'The Muslim is the brother of another Muslim, it is not permissible for a Muslim to sell his brother goods in which there is a defect, without pointing that out to him.'"[8]

---

4. Selling old gold with new gold and adding a fee.

This is giving more in return for less of the same commodity, and this is from usury. Gold and silver and that which takes its place it not permissible to sell, unless it is hand to hand and like gold for like

[6] **Translator's note:** Ibn 'Umar said, "The Prophet ﷺ forbade selling the offspring of the offspring of a pregnant animal." (*Sunan an-Nasā'ī* 4624)

[7] *Ṣaḥīḥ Muslim* 101

[8] *Sunan Ibn Mājah*

gold. It is the same whether it is gold coins or molded, as long as it remains gold. It is not affected by being molded. The Prophet ﷺ said:

لا تَبِيعُوا الذَّهَبَ بِالذَّهَبِ إِلا مِثْلًا بِمِثْلٍ وَلا تُشِفُّوا بَعْضَهَا عَلَى بَعْضٍ.

"Do not sell gold for gold except like for like, and do not let the quantities differ."[9]

In *Ṣaḥīḥ Muslim* the wording is:

لاَ تَبِيعُوا الذَّهَبَ بِالذَّهَبِ وَلاَ الْوَرِقَ بِالْوَرِقِ إِلاَّ وَزْنًا بِوَزْنٍ مِثْلاً بِمِثْلٍ سَوَاءً بِسَوَاءٍ.

"Do not sell gold for gold and silver for silver weight for weight or of the same quality."[10]

Whoever wants to buy new gold and they have old molded gold, then let them sell the old gold for a price, and once he has the money in his hand he can buy the gold from wherever he likes, whether it is molded or not.

---

5. Completing two transactions in one.

This transaction is prohibited based upon what has been narrated from Abū Hurayrah ﷺ; he said that the Messenger of Allāh ﷺ said:

مَنْ بَاعَ بَيْعَتَيْنِ فِي بَيْعَةٍ فَلَهُ أَوْكَسُهُمَا أَوِ الرِّبَا.

"If anyone makes two transactions combined in one bargain, he should have the lesser of the two or it will involve usury."[11]

Abū Hurayrah ﷺ said:

---

[9] Collected in *Al-Bukhārī* and *Muslim* from the *ḥadīth* of Sa'eed al-Khudri.

[10] *Ṣaḥīḥ Muslim* 1584

[11] *Sunan Abī Dāwūd* 3461

نَهَى رَسُولُ اللَّهِ صَلَّى اللَّهُ عَلَيْهِ وَسَلَّمَ عَنْ بَيْعَتَيْنِ فِي بَيْعَةٍ.

"The Messenger of Allāh ﷺ forbade two transactions in one."[12]

Ibn al-Qayyim رحمه الله said: "This is when the person says 'I will sell you this merchandise for ten in cash or for twenty in installments, this is an *'Eenah* transaction[13]. This is the meaning of the *ḥadīth*. If the intent is immediate cash for deferred cash, then he only deserves to accept the principle amount, and it is the lower of the two prices. If he takes the higher of the two prices then he has accepted interest. And there is no way around one of two scenarios, either he takes the lower of the two prices or he takes interest. And this narration cannot be understood in any other way."

---

6. Selling impermissible merchandise, such as cigarettes, magazines with pictures of women, cigarette advertisements, indecent films, machines and devices which are used for impermissible acts, or the selling of books that contain passion or lowly ideologies.

The scholars have said that selling items like those mentioned in not permissible. The tribulation caused by magazines and movies is tremendous, and its prohibition is clear. Allāh the Exalted said:

﴿ يَا أَيُّهَا النَّبِيُّ قُل لِّأَزْوَاجِكَ وَبَنَاتِكَ وَنِسَاءِ الْمُؤْمِنِينَ
يُدْنِينَ عَلَيْهِنَّ مِن جَلَابِيبِهِنَّ ﴾

O Prophet! Tell your wives and your daughters and the women of the believers to draw their cloaks (veils)

[12] *At-Tirmidhī* 985

[13] **Translator's note:** To sell something for a price to be paid at a later date, then to buy it back for a lower price to be paid immediately. The buyer acquires cash and will pay back a higher amount after a while, so it is as if it is a loan in the form of a sale.

all over their bodies

[Sūrah al-Aḥzāb 33:59]

This is because she calls to indecency. Allāh the Exalted said:

﴿ إِنَّ الَّذِينَ يُحِبُّونَ أَن تَشِيعَ الْفَاحِشَةُ فِي الَّذِينَ آمَنُوا لَهُمْ عَذَابٌ أَلِيمٌ فِي الدُّنْيَا وَالْآخِرَةِ ۚ وَاللَّهُ يَعْلَمُ وَأَنتُمْ لَا تَعْلَمُونَ ﴾

Verily, those who like that (the crime of) illegal sexual intercourse should be propagated among those who believe, they will have a painful torment in this world and in the Hereafter. And Allāh knows and you know not.

[Sūrah an-Nūr 24:19]

The Messenger of Allāh ﷺ said:

الْمَرْأَةُ عَوْرَةٌ فَإِذَا خَرَجَتِ اسْتَشْرَفَهَا الشَّيْطَانُ.

"The woman is *'awrah* (that which should be covered) when she goes out Shaytān raises the glances towards her."[14]

So how about those enchanting seductive pictures of the disbelieving women?! The prohibition of this is known by way of the evidence and the consensus of the scholars, therefore the money earned from this is likewise unlawful. The Prophet ﷺ said:

إن الله إذا حرَّم شيئاً حرَّم ثمنه.

"When Allāh forbids a thing, He also forbids its price."[15]

Consequently, to consume an unlawful earning is to consume filth and that which is impermissible.

[14] *Jāmi' at-Tirmidhī* 1173

[15] Collected by Abū Dāwūd 3488

We ask Allāh for safety and security.

---

7. Selling music cassettes and videos which contain images of women, corrupt ideologies, and indecency.

This affair has been clarified in the 6th affair.

---

8. Artificially inflating prices; this is to offer the seller more than the selling price without having an intention to purchase the product.

Ibn 'Umar 🙵 said:

أَنَّ رَسُولَ اللَّهِ صلى الله عليه وسلم نَهَى عَنِ النَّجْشِ.

"The Prophet forbade artificially inflating[16] prices."[17]

---

9. The sale of a Muslim over the sale of his brother.

For example this is to say to a person who is selling merchandise for ten riyals "I will buy it from you for twelve riyals." Or if a person buys a product for eight riyals, so another man says I will sell you the same product for six riyals. This is not permissible and this is a reason for brothers turn their back on each other, boycotting each other and envy. Abū Hurayrah 🙵 said, the Prophet 🙵 said:

لاَ يَبِيعُ الرَّجُلُ عَلَى بَيْعِ أَخِيهِ.

---

[16] **Translator's note:** Abū Isa At-Tirmidhī said: "An-Najsh is when a man who knows about the goods comes to the owner of the goods to offer him more than what it is worth, doing so in the presence of the buyer. He intends to seduce the buyer while he himself does not want to buy it, rather he only wants to deceive the buyer with his offer. And this is type of deceit." (*Jāmi' at-Tirmidhī* 1304)

[17] *Sunan an-Nasā'ī* 4505

"No man should sell over the sale of his brother."[18]

---

10. Deception and fraud in sales.

Deception is not permissible. The Prophet ﷺ said:

مَنْ غَشَّنَا فَلَيْسَ مِنَّا.

"Whoever deceives us is not from us."[19]

Likewise fraud is prohibited and not permissible. This is proven by the statement of the Prophet ﷺ:

لاَ تُصَرُّوا الإِبِلَ وَالْغَنَمَ.

"Do not tie the udders of camels or sheep."[20]

The meaning of fraud is to beautify a product you want to sell at the time of sell while concealing a defect in order to sell the merchandise.

---

11. Using false oaths to promote merchandise.

Using false oaths removes the blessings from the sale. The Prophet ﷺ said:

الْيَمِينُ الْفَاجِرَةُ مَنْفَقَةٌ لِلسِّلْعَةِ مَمْحَقَةٌ لِلْكَسْبِ.

"The false oath is beneficial for the sale, but it removes the blessings from the earnings."[21]

Allāh the Exalted said:

---

[18] *Sunan an-Nasā'ī* 4506

[19] *Ṣaḥīḥ Muslim* 101

[20] *Ṣaḥīḥ Muslim* 1515

[21] Agreed upon by al-Bukhārī and Muslim

﴿ إِنَّ الَّذِينَ يَشْتَرُونَ بِعَهْدِ اللَّهِ وَأَيْمَانِهِمْ ثَمَنًا قَلِيلًا أُولَٰئِكَ لَا خَلَاقَ لَهُمْ فِي الْآخِرَةِ وَلَا يُكَلِّمُهُمُ اللَّهُ وَلَا يَنظُرُ إِلَيْهِمْ يَوْمَ الْقِيَامَةِ وَلَا يُزَكِّيهِمْ وَلَهُمْ عَذَابٌ أَلِيمٌ ﴾

Verily, those who purchase a small gain at the cost of Allāh's Covenant and their oaths, they shall have no portion in the Hereafter. Neither will Allāh speak to them, nor look at them on the Day of Resurrection, nor will He purify them, and they shall have a painful torment.

[Sūrah Āli 'Imrān 3:77]

The Messenger of Allāh ﷺ said:

ثَلَاثَةٌ لَا يُكَلِّمُهُمْ اللَّهُ يَوْمَ الْقِيَامَةِ وَلَا يَنْظُرُ إِلَيْهِمْ وَلَا يُزَكِّيهِمْ وَلَهُمْ عَذَابٌ أَلِيمٌ قَالَ فَقَرَأَهَا رَسُولُ اللَّهِ صَلَّى اللَّهُ عَلَيْهِ وَسَلَّمَ ثَلَاثَ مِرَارًا قَالَ أَبُو ذَرٍّ خَابُوا وَخَسِرُوا مَنْ هُمْ يَا رَسُولَ اللَّهِ قَالَ الْمُسْبِلُ وَالْمَنَّانُ وَالْمُنَفِّقُ سِلْعَتَهُ بِالْحَلِفِ الْكَاذِبِ.

"There are three to whom Allāh will not speak on the Day of Resurrection, nor will He look at them or purify them, and theirs will be a severe torment." The Messenger of Allāh ﷺ repeated it three times. Abū Dharr said, "They are lost and doomed. Who are they, O Messenger of Allāh?" He said, "The one who lets his garment hang below his ankles, the one who reminds others of his favor, and the one who sells his product by means of false oaths."[22]

The narrations proving the prohibition of false oaths and how they remove the blessing from the sale are numerous.

---

[22] *Ṣaḥīḥ Muslim* 102

12. Lack of concern with learning the rules and regulations of business transactions.

Many of the Muslims are lackadaisical in regard to learning the rules and regulations. Not learning the rules and regulations could lead to consuming impermissible wealth, invalid transactions, and acquisition of wealth which is unlawful. It is incumbent upon the merchant to learn the principles of buying and selling so he will bc from the successful.

It has been narrated that 'Umar ﷺ used to go around the market place hitting some of the merchants with a switch while saying: "No one should sell in our market except for the one who has understanding of the religion, if not then he will consume usury willingly or unwillingly."

And in another narration, 'Umar ﷺ said:

لاْ يَبعْ فِيْ سُوْقِنَا إِلاْ مَنْ قَدْ تَفَقَّهَ فِيْ الدِّيْنِ.

"No one should sell in our marketplace except those who have knowledge of the religion."[23]

[23] *At-Tirmidhī* 487

12

Common Mistakes Among Men

1. The youth resembling the West in their dress and hairstyles.

Imitating the disbelievers in matter which are particular to them such as clothing and general physical appearance is prohibited. The Prophet ﷺ said:

مَنْ تَشَبَّهَ بِقَوْمٍ، فَهُوَ مِنْهُمْ.

"Whoever resembles a people is from them."[1]

As it relates to clothing; the Prophet ﷺ forbade the Muslims from wearing the garments of the disbelievers. 'Abdullāh bin Amr bin al-Aws said:

رَأَى رَسُولُ اللَّهِ صَلَّى اللَّهُ عَلَيْهِ وَسَلَّمَ عَلَيَّ ثَوْبَيْنِ مُعَصْفَرَيْنِ فَقَالَ إِنَّ هَذِهِ مِنْ ثِيَابِ الْكُفَّارِ فَلَا تَلْبَسْهَا.

"The Messenger of Allāh ﷺ saw me wearing two garments dyed with safflower and said: 'These are garments of the disbelieves; so do not

[1] Abū Dāwūd 4031

wear them.'"[2]

This proves wearing clothes particular to the disbelievers in not permissible. In *Ṣaḥīḥ al-Bukhārī* and *Ṣaḥīḥ Muslim* it states:

أن النبي صلى الله عليه وسلم خالف أهل الكتاب في سدل الشعر.

"The Prophet ﷺ opposed the way of the People of the Book in regard to leaving the hair loose."[3]

Imitating them in matter specific to them falls upon the general meaning of the statement of the Prophet ﷺ:

مَنْ تَشَبَّهَ بِقَوْمٍ، فَهُوَ مِنْهُمْ.

"Whoever resembles a people is from them."[4]

The scholars have stated this narration necessitates the prohibition of imitating the disbelievers in matters particular to them, likewise it is understood that imitating the pagans is prohibited and we are commanded to differ from them.

---

2. Allowing sports to distract them from the prayer and other obligations.

This is due to weak faith or its disappearance. Allāh the Exalted said:

﴿ فَخَلَفَ مِن بَعْدِهِمْ خَلْفٌ أَضَاعُوا الصَّلَاةَ وَاتَّبَعُوا الشَّهَوَاتِ ۖ فَسَوْفَ يَلْقَوْنَ غَيًّا ﴾

Then, there has succeeded them a posterity who have given up the prayers and followed lusts. So they will

[2] *Muslim* 2077

[3] Collected in al-*Bukhārī* and Muslim

[4] *Abū Dāwūd* 4031

be thrown in Hell.

[Sūrah Maryam 19:59]

Prayer is a pillar of the religion. It must be given precedence over every desire and game. It is established during its proper time. Allāh has threaten those who are apathetic towards the prayer, thus they do not remember it because it does not hold a high regard with them. He said:

﴿ فَوَيْلٌ لِّلْمُصَلِّينَ ۝٤ ٱلَّذِينَ هُمْ عَن صَلَاتِهِمْ سَاهُونَ ۝٥ ﴾

So woe to those who pray, those who delay their prayer from their stated fixed times

[Sūrah al-Mā'ūn 107:4-5]

It is obligatory upon whoever hears the call to prayer to respond to it (by attending the prayer) and to not become preoccupied and distracted from the prayer with play, business or the like.

---

3. Listening to the impermissible, watching indecency, and reading magazines and destructive newspapers.

---

4. Wearing tight and transparent clothing, growing the mustache, and shaving the beard.

---

5. Traveling abroad and traveling to practice lowly vices.

---

6. Using musical instruments.

These affairs have been previously clarified, and warned against. Its rules and proofs have been mentioned. May Allāh have mercy upon the slave who seeks safety and abandons sins and performed the obligations.

13

Corrupters of the Ears & Eyes

---

1. Reading magazines, books, and newspapers that encourage wickedness and that which opposes Islamic legislation and destroys good character.

---

2. Watching romance and detective movies and plays, which grow wickedness and a love of crime.

---

3. Wasting time watching soccer matches and wrestling. which have no point.

---

4. Listening to singers and music.

It is known by the legislative texts that these four matters are prohibited, and the proof has been separately mentioned. Allāh the Exalted said:

﴿ إِنَّ السَّمْعَ وَالْبَصَرَ وَالْفُؤَادَ كُلُّ أُولَـٰئِكَ كَانَ عَنْهُ مَسْئُولًا ﴾

Verily! The hearing, and the sight, and the heart, of each of those you will be questioned (by Allāh).

[Sūrah al-Isrā' 17:36]

Watching pictures that show the *'awrah* of men (area of the body which should be covered) such as wrestling, or shows which reveal the *'awrah* of women such as movies and soap operas is prohibited. It is incumbent to avoid this. Likewise listening to music, the proof that it is impermissible has already been mentioned. It is likewise obligatory to abandon reading books which don't benefit the Muslims, in order to safeguard his religion, seeking the afterlife, and seeking safety from sins and its effects.

As for watching soccer matches, if it distracts them from the prayer and obligations then it is prohibited. If it does not divert them from the prayer and does not contain anything prohibited, it is still better to abandon watching these matches.

Many of them have a type of sports fanaticism and loyalty for other than Allāh and aspects of the Pre-Islamic Days of Ignorance.

---

5. Being lackadaisical towards enjoining the good and forbidding the evil.

Enjoining the good and forbidding the evil is incumbent upon every Muslim according to their ability. These are the keys to good for this *ummah*.

﴿ كُنتُمْ خَيْرَ أُمَّةٍ أُخْرِجَتْ لِلنَّاسِ تَأْمُرُونَ بِالْمَعْرُوفِ وَتَنْهَوْنَ عَنِ الْمُنكَرِ وَتُؤْمِنُونَ بِاللَّهِ ﴾

You are the best of peoples ever raised up for mankind; you enjoin the good and forbid the evil, and you believe in Allāh.

[Sūrah Āli 'Imrān 3:110]

Showing apathy towards enjoining the good is not permissible, rather abandoning it and showing apathy towards it is a reason for the curse of Allāh, His Anger and it allows His punishment to befall those who do so. Allāh the Exalted said:

﴿ لُعِنَ الَّذِينَ كَفَرُوا مِن بَنِي إِسْرَائِيلَ عَلَىٰ لِسَانِ دَاوُودَ وَعِيسَى ابْنِ مَرْيَمَ ۚ ذَٰلِكَ بِمَا عَصَوا وَّكَانُوا يَعْتَدُونَ ﴿٧٨﴾ كَانُوا لَا يَتَنَاهَوْنَ عَن مُّنكَرٍ فَعَلُوهُ ۚ لَبِئْسَ مَا كَانُوا يَفْعَلُونَ ﴿٧٩﴾ ﴾

> Those among the Children of Israel who disbelieved were cursed by the tongue of Dāwūd and Jesus son of Maryam. That was because they disobeyed and were ever transgressing beyond bounds. They used not to forbid one another from the evil which they committed. Vile indeed was what they used to do.
>
> *[Sūrah al-Mā'idah 5:78-79]*

The Muslim *ummah* calls towards good and enjoins the good. This is what Allāh has commanded and the good results of this are known by the legislation. Abandoning enjoining the good and forbidding the evil is a reason for the supplication to be rejected. Thus the people will supplicate and will not be answered. This is a great calamity, as none of us are independent of needing Allāh even for the blink of an eye. The Messenger of Allāh ﷺ said:

لَتَأْمُرُنَّ بِالْمَعْرُوفِ وَلَتَنْهَوُنَّ عَنْ الْمُنْكَرِ أَوْ لَيُوشِكَنَّ اللَّهُ عَزَّ وَجَلَّ أَنْ يَبْعَثَ عَلَيْكُمْ عَذَابًا مِنْ عِنْدِهِ ثُمَّ تَدْعُونَهُ فَلَا يُسْتَجَابُ لَكُمْ.

"Either you command good and forbid evil, or Allāh will soon send upon you a punishment from Him, then you will call upon Him, but He will not respond to you."[1]

It is obligatory for those who are enjoined to good and forbidden from evil to obey the command of Allāh and His Messenger. And

[1] *Jāmi' at-Tirmidhī* 2169

they must understand that those who enjoin them to good only want good for them and safety. They love that they should earn good deeds and elevate in degrees. Thus they must accept this advice with appreciation, perchance Allāh will forgive and pardon them.

14

Mistakes Related to Travel

---

1. Traveling abroad for vacation and what accompanies it from neglecting obligations and using the impermissible.

This is obvious evil, and clearly impermissible. Traveling to lands where polytheism, evil, and allowance of prohibited actions is present is not permissible except due to necessity; for those whom are able to display their religion and openly display the truth and *tawheed*. As for traveling accompanied by sin and leaving off the obligations, and not openly displaying the religion; no scholar has said this is permissible. This is a calamity. Those who are saved are those whom Allāh saves.

---

2. Befriending the disbelievers and imitating them in actions and speech.

Allāh the Exalted said:

﴿لَّا تَجِدُ قَوْمًا يُؤْمِنُونَ بِاللَّهِ وَالْيَوْمِ الْآخِرِ يُوَادُّونَ مَنْ حَادَّ
اللَّهَ وَرَسُولَهُ وَلَوْ كَانُوا آبَاءَهُمْ أَوْ أَبْنَاءَهُمْ أَوْ إِخْوَانَهُمْ أَوْ

عَشِيرَتَهُمْ ﴾

You will not find any people who believe in Allāh
and the Last Day, making friendship with those who
oppose Allāh and His Messenger, even though they
were their fathers, or their sons, or their brothers, or
their kindred (people).

[Sūrah al-Mujādila 58:22]

Befriending the disbelievers negates faith, either completely or
according to the situation. It is obligatory to break the connection
of friendship because the enemies of Allāh, His legislation, and His
religion; are loved or befriended by those who love Allāh and His
Messenger. How wonderful is the statement of Ibn al-Qayyim ﷦!

أتحــب أعـداء الحـبيب وتـدعي، حبــا لــه مــا ذاك فـي إمكـان.

"Do you love the enemies of the beloved (Prophet Muḥammad) while
claiming to love him? That is not possible!"

As for imitating them in their actions and speech, this issue has
already been clarified. It is not permissible based upon the statement
of the Prophet ﷺ:

مَنْ تَشَبَّهَ بِقَوْمٍ، فَهُوَ مِنْهُمْ.

"Whoever resembles a people is from them."[1]

---

3. Not giving *da'wah* in the lands of disbelief and not displaying the beauty of Islām.

Displaying the religion of Islām is from the conditions which allow
travel to the lands of the pagans. Therefore the person who is not able
to do that is not permitted to travel there. The Muslim is required
to perfect his religion and increase his faith by inviting people to

---

[1] *Abū Dāwūd* 4031

Islām and openly displaying his religion wherever he may be. This is more so need in the lands of disbelief. This is from the guidance of the Companions of the Prophet ﷺ and those that followed them. They entered the lands of disbelief inviting them to Islām. Thus Allāh benefited a large number of people by way of them. May Allāh be pleased with them.

---

4. Defaming the Muslims by committing evil actions, and the evil manners of some Muslims abroad.

The Muslim is an example, and he is not representing himself, rather he is representing his religion and the *ummah* of Muslims as a whole. Perhaps he will prevent some people who want to enter Islām due to their behavior and their representation of the religion.

---

5. Encouraging the Muslims to travel abroad and praising the lands of disbelief and their actions.

These individuals call to sin, thus they will incur the sin and the sin of those who work according to their encouragement. The Prophet ﷺ said:

مَنْ دَعَا إِلَى هُدًى كَانَ لَهُ مِنَ الأَجْرِ مِثْلُ أُجُورِ مَنْ تَبِعَهُ لاَ يَنْقُصُ ذَلِكَ مِنْ أُجُورِهِمْ شَيْئًا وَمَنْ دَعَا إِلَى ضَلاَلَةٍ كَانَ عَلَيْهِ مِنَ الإِثْمِ مِثْلُ آثَامِ مَنْ تَبِعَهُ لاَ يَنْقُصُ ذَلِكَ مِنْ آثَامِهِمْ شَيْئًا.

"Whoever calls others to guidance will have a reward like that of those who follow it, without that detracting from their reward in the slightest. And whoever calls others to misguidance will have a burden of sin like that of those who follow it, without it detracting from their burden in the slightest."[2]

---

[2] *Muslim* 2674

The Messenger of Allāh ﷺ said:

وَمَنْ سَنَّ فِي الْإِسْلَامِ سُنَّةً سَيِّئَةً فَعُمِلَ بِهَا بَعْدَهُ كُتِبَ عَلَيْهِ مِثْلُ وِزْرِ مَنْ عَمِلَ بِهَا، وَلَا يَنْقُصُ مِنْ أَوْزَارِهِمْ شَيْءٌ.

"And whoever introduces a bad precedent in Islām will bear the burden of sin for that, and the burden of those who do it after him, without that detracting from their burden in the slightest."[3]

---

6. Muslim women being lackadaisical in regard to wearing *ḥijāb* and uncovering when they travel abroad

The evidence for this issue was previously presented for the obligation for the woman to cover and safeguard all of her body. We have heard of some of the Muslim women abandoning their *ḥijāb* when they arrive to a country which is not their native country. The reason is the absence of truly venerating faith, and forsaking obedience of Allāh and obedience of His Messenger concerning the *ḥijāb*. Allāh is the object of worship and obeyed in every place and location, thus the women and men must obey Him in their homeland and abroad.

﴿ إِنَّ اللَّهَ كَانَ عَلَيْكُمْ رَقِيبًا ﴾

Surely, Allāh is Ever an All-Watcher over you.

[Sūrah an-Nisā' 4:1]

Any women desiring safety from the Hellfire and the punishment of the grave must obey Allāh and adhere to His commands and obligations. She must avoid uncovering and revealing herself. How many faces revealed and shins uncovered will be scorched by the Hellfire in the grave and on the Day of Judgment!

Any women desiring Paradise let her rush towards it by obedience and adhering to the *ḥijāb* and covering. The devoted, chaste women;

[3] *Muslim* 1017

their abode is Paradise and the pleasure of the Most Merciful.

Don't be frightened by the many who fall into sin, because those who will be saved are always few in number.

﴿ وَإِن تُطِعْ أَكْثَرَ مَن فِي الْأَرْضِ يُضِلُّوكَ عَن سَبِيلِ اللَّهِ ﴾

And if you obey most of those on earth, they will mislead you far away from Allāh's Path.

[Sūrah al-An'ām 6:116]

﴿ وَمَا آمَنَ مَعَهُ إِلَّا قَلِيلٌ ﴾

And none believed with him, except a few.

[Sūrah Hūd 11:40]

15

Mistakes Related to Keeping the Ties of Kinship

1. Not visiting the relatives.

This perhaps can be considered breaking the ties of kinship and the Muslim is commanded to uphold the ties of kinship. The Messenger of Allāh ﷺ said:

مَنْ كَانَ يُؤْمِنُ بِاللَّهِ وَالْيَوْمِ الْآخِرِ فَلْيَصِلْ رَحِمَهُ.

"Whoever believes in Allāh and the last day let him maintain the ties of kinship."[1]

Keeping the ties of kinship results in reward, increased provisions, and prolonging the life span. In the *ḥadīth* of Anas in Malik ﷺ, the Messenger of Allāh ﷺ said:

مَنْ سَرَّهُ أَنْ يُبْسَطَ لَهُ فِي رِزْقِهِ أَوْ يُنْسَأَ لَهُ فِي أَثَرِهِ فَلْيَصِلْ رَحِمَهُ.

"Whoever loves that his provision is increased, and his life span

[1] *Ṣaḥīḥ al-Bukhārī* 6138

prolonged then let him maintain the ties of kinship."[2]

Not keeping the ties of kinship is to break the ties of kinship. Allāh the Exalted said:

﴿ فَهَلْ عَسَيْتُمْ إِن تَوَلَّيْتُمْ أَن تُفْسِدُوا فِي الْأَرْضِ وَتُقَطِّعُوا أَرْحَامَكُمْ ﴿٢٢﴾ أُولَٰئِكَ الَّذِينَ لَعَنَهُمُ اللَّهُ فَأَصَمَّهُمْ وَأَعْمَىٰ أَبْصَارَهُمْ ﴿٢٣﴾ ﴾

Would you then, if you were given the authority, do mischief in the land, and sever your ties of kinship? Such are they whom Allāh has cursed, so that He has made them deaf and blinded their sight.

[Sūrah Muḥammad 47:22-23]

It was narrated from 'Ā'ishah ﵂ that the Messenger of Allāh ﷺ said:

الرَّحِمُ مُعَلَّقَةٌ بِالْعَرْشِ، تَقُولُ: مَنْ وَصَلَنِي وَصَلَهُ اللَّهُ، وَمَنْ قَطَعَنِي قَطَعَهُ اللَّهُ.

"The womb is suspended from the Throne. It says: Whoever connects me, Allāh will connect them, and whoever severs me Allāh will sever him."[3]

This is sufficient as an incitement to maintain the ties of kinship and sufficient as a threat against severing the ties of kinship.

---

2. Cutting off the relatives and boycotting them for the smallest reasons.

Boycotting without a legislative reason is not allowable; rather keeping the ties of kinship is obligatory even if your relatives harm

[2] *Ṣaḥīḥ al-Bukhārī* 5986

[3] *Ṣaḥīḥ Muslim* 2555

you in your person. The person who truly keeps the ties of kinship is the one who connects with his relatives although they distance themselves from him. The Prophet ﷺ said:

لَيْسَ الْوَاصِلُ بِالْمُكَافِئِ؛ وَلَكِنْ الْوَاصِلُ الَّذِي إِذَا قُطِعَتْ رَحِمُهُ وَصَلَهَ.

"The one who maintains a relationship with his relatives only because they maintain a relationship with him is not truly upholding the ties of kinship. The one who truly upholds those ties is the one who does so even if they break off their relationship with him."[4]

Abū Hurayrah ﷺ said:

أَنَّ رَجُلًا قَالَ: يَا رَسُولَ اللَّهِ! إِنَّ لِي قَرَابَةً أَصِلُهُمْ وَيَقْطَعُونِي، وَأُحْسِنُ إِلَيْهِمْ وَيُسِيئُونَ إِلَيَّ، وَأَحْلُمُ عَنْهُمْ وَيَجْهَلُونَ عَلَيَّ؟ فَقَالَ: لَئِنْ كُنْتَ كَمَا قُلْتَ فَكَأَنَّمَا تُسِفُّهُمُ الْمَلَّ، وَلَا يَزَالُ مَعَكَ مِنَ اللَّهِ ظَهِيرٌ عَلَيْهِمْ مَا دُمْتَ عَلَى ذَلِكَ.

"A man said, 'O Messenger of Allāh, I have relatives with whom I try to keep in touch, but they cut me off. I treat them well, but they abuse me. I am patient and kind towards them, but they insult me.' He ﷺ said, 'If you are as you say, then it is as if you are putting hot ashes in their mouths. Allāh will continue to support you as long as you continue to do that.'"[5]

---

3. Not acquainting oneself with his relatives and not calling them by phone if you are not able to visit them.

---

4. Being heedless concerning poor relatives and not assisting them financially and acting kind towards them.

---

[4] *Al-Bukhārī* 5645

[5] *Muslim* 2558

Allāh the Exalted said:

﴿ وَلَا يَأْتَلِ أُولُو الْفَضْلِ مِنكُمْ وَالسَّعَةِ أَن يُؤْتُوا أُولِي الْقُرْبَىٰ وَالْمَسَاكِينَ وَالْمُهَاجِرِينَ فِي سَبِيلِ اللَّهِ ۖ وَلْيَعْفُوا وَلْيَصْفَحُوا ۗ أَلَا تُحِبُّونَ أَن يَغْفِرَ اللَّهُ لَكُمْ ۗ وَاللَّهُ غَفُورٌ رَّحِيمٌ ﴾

And let not those among you who are blessed with graces and wealth swear not to give (any sort of help) to their kinsmen, the poor, and those who left their homes for Allāh's Cause. Let them pardon and forgive. Do you not love that Allāh should forgive you? And Allāh is Oft-Forgiving, Most Merciful.

[Sūrah an-Nūr 24:22]

The Prophet ﷺ said:

الصَّدَقَةُ عَلَى الْمِسْكِينِ صَدَقَةٌ، وَعَلَى ذِي الْقَرَابَةِ اثْنَتَانِ صَدَقَةٌ وَصِلَةٌ.

"Charity given to a poor person is charity, but charity given to a relative is two things: charity and upholding the ties of kinship."[6]

Bahz bin Hakim narrated from his father that his grandfather said:

قُلْتُ يَا رَسُولَ اللَّهِ مَنْ أَبَرُّ قَالَ أُمَّكَ ثُمَّ أُمَّكَ ثُمَّ أُمَّكَ ثُمَّ أَبَاكَ ثُمَّ الأَقْرَبَ فَالأَقْرَبَ.

"I said, 'O Messenger of Allāh, to whom should I show kindness?' He replied, 'Your mother, then your mother, then your mother, and then comes your father, and then your relatives in order of relationship.'"[7]

---

[6] *At-Tirmidhī* 658 and *Ibn Mājah* 1844

[7] *Sunan Abī Dāwūd* 5139

5. Apathy towards spending upon those relatives upon whom it is mandatory to spend.

It is obligatory to spend upon the relatives if they do not have anyone to spend upon them, and if they are from the inheritors. Allāh the Exalted said:

﴿ وَعَلَى الْوَارِثِ مِثْلُ ذَٰلِكَ ﴾

And on the (father's) heir is incumbent the like of that (which was incumbent on the father).[8]

[Sūrah al-Baqarah 2:233]

Even if they are not heirs, it is recommended to spend upon them according to one's ability and there is a great deal of virtue and benefit in this. The Messenger of Allāh ﷺ said:

ابْدَأْ بِمَنْ تَعُولُ، أُمَّكَ وَأَبَاكَ، وَأُخْتَكَ وَأَخَاكَ، ثُمَّ أَدْنَاكَ أَدْنَاكَ.

"Begin with those under your care; your mother, your father, your sister, your brother, and then those next closest to you."[9]

His statement "your mother" means give to your mother.

[8] Translation by Mushin Khan

[9] *Sunan an-Nasā'ī* 2532

16

Mistakes Related to Marriage

1. Apathy in regard to choosing a woman.

From the things which the person seeking marriage must be diligent upon is seeking a religious woman who will help him uphold the commands and obedience of Allāh. The Prophet ﷺ command us with this in his statement:

تُنْكَحُ الْمَرْأَةُ لِأَرْبَعٍ: لِمَالِهَا، وَلِحَسَبِهَا، وَلِجَمَالِهَا، وَلِدِينِهَا، فَاظْفَرْ بِذَاتِ الدِّينِ تَرِبَتْ يَدَاكَ.

"A woman is married for four things: her wealth, her lineage, her beauty and her religious commitment. Seek the one who is religiously-committed, may your hands be rubbed with dust (i.e., may you prosper)."[1]

2. The man who proposes to a woman without looking at her in the prescribed manner.

[1] *Al-Bukhārī* 4802 and *Muslim* 1466

It is prescribed for the man who proposes to a woman to look at what is predominantly seen of her such as her face and hands. And he ponders over her and what incites him to marry her. This is based upon the statement of the Prophet ﷺ to the man who wants to marry a woman:

انْظُرْ إِلَيْهَا.

"Look at her."[2]

And the Messenger of Allāh ﷺ said:

إِذَا خَطَبَ أَحَدُكُمْ امْرَأَةً فَلا جُنَاحَ عَلَيْهِ أَنْ يَنْظُرَ إِلَيْهَا إِذَا كَانَ، إِنَّمَا يَنْظُرُ إِلَيْهَا لِخِطْبَةٍ، فَإِنَّهُ يَنْظُرُ إِلَيْهَا وَإِنْ كَانَتْ لا تَعْلَمُ.

"If one of you proposes to a woman, there is no harm upon him if he looks at her, if he is only looking at her to propose to her. Then he can look at her even if she is not aware of this."[3]

It is not allowed for a man to look at a woman if he does not want to propose to her. Likewise he does not look at her in seclusion, or without decency. It is only allowed to look at her without her knowledge or with her knowledge and her family's knowledge if his looking is for the purpose of marriage. It is not allowed for the family to expose their daughters under the guise of a proposal and this is not done by those who have jealousy for their family. It is only allowed for the man to look if he is known to be sincere about seeking her for marriage or after the proposal. And Allāh knows best.

---

3. Delaying marriage until after studies.

This is in contrast to what the Muslim has been commanded with in regards to guarding their chastity and guarding themselves. Early

[2] Collected by Muslim

[3] Collected by Aḥmad

marriage—in most cases—brings about a healthy body, healthy intellect and ease of the soul. The Prophet ﷺ said:

يَا مَعْشَرَ الشَّبَابِ مَنْ اسْتَطَاعَ منكم الْبَاءَةَ فَلْيَتَزَوَّجْ، فَإِنَّهُ أَغَضُّ لِلْبَصَرِ، وَأَحْصَنُ لِلْفَرْجِ، وَمَنْ لَمْ يَسْتَطِعْ فَعَلَيْهِ بِالصَّوْمِ فَإِنَّهُ لَهُ وِجَاءٌ.

"O young men, whoever among you can afford it, let him get married, for it is more effective in lowering the gaze and guarding one's chastity. And whoever cannot afford it should fast, for it will be a shield for him."[4]

As for men and women delaying marriage until after studies, this is a strange affair, thrown upon us from those who are not from us. This practice is unknown to the Islamic nation. If the young men are able to afford marriage, they are of sound intellect, they will treat the women kindly, then it is recommended for men like this to marry and in some cases it may be obligatory. The same applies to the young woman; early marriage is medicine for both sexes, especially during this day and time.

---

4. Excessively high *mahr* (dowry).

The principle is that there is not restriction on the dowry, but an outrageously high dowry is in opposition to the Prophetic guidance. Likewise it is a path which leads towards aversion of marriage, thus it is necessary to close this door. It is upon the guardians of the women to lower the dowry, and to select righteous men for those women under their care. The dowry given by the Prophet ﷺ to his wives was Twelve and a half *uqiyah* as stated in *Ṣaḥīḥ Muslim*[5].

[4] *Al-Bukhārī* 5066 and *Muslim* 1400

[5] **Translator's note:** Abū Salamah bin 'Abdul-Rahman said: "I asked Ā'ishah the wife of the Prophet ﷺ what the mahr given by the Prophet ﷺ was. She said: 'The mahr that he gave to his wives was twelve uqiyah and a nashsh.' She said, Do you know what a nashsh is? I replied: 'No.' She said it is half of an *ooqiyah*. That was five hundred dirhams. This was the mahr given by the Prophet be upon him to his wives." (*Muslim* 1426)

'Umar bin al-Khattāb ﷺ said:

لا تُغَالُوا صَدَاقَ النِّسَاءِ فَإِنَّهَا لَوْ كَانَتْ مَكْرُمَةً فِي الدُّنْيَا أَوْ تَقْوَى عِنْدَ اللَّهِ كَانَ أَوْلاكُمْ وَأَحَقَّكُمْ بِهَا مُحَمَّدٌ صَلَّى اللَّهُ عَلَيْهِ وَسَلَّمَ مَا أَصْدَقَ امْرَأَةً مِنْ نِسَائِهِ وَلا أُصْدِقَتْ امْرَأَةٌ مِنْ بَنَاتِهِ أَكْثَرَ مِنْ اثْنَتَيْ عَشْرَةَ أُوقِيَّةً وَإِنَّ الرَّجُلَ لَيُثَقِّلُ صَدَقَةَ امْرَأَتِهِ حَتَّى يَكُونَ لَهَا عَدَاوَةٌ فِي نَفْسِهِ وَيَقُولُ قَدْ كَلِفْتُ إِلَيْكِ عَلَقَ الْقِرْبَةِ.

"Do not go to extremes in regard to the dowries of women, for if that were a sign of honor and dignity in this world or a sign of piety before Allāh, then Muḥammad ﷺ would have been more deserving than you to do this. But he did not give any of his wives, and none of his daughters were given, more than twelve *uqiyah*. A man may increase the dowry until he feels resentment against her and says, 'You cost me everything I own, and caused me a great deal of hardship.'"[6]

---

5. Carrying a woman on a platform amongst women when her husband is with her.

This carries two prohibitions:

1) Resembling the disbelievers in carrying the spouses on a platform by joining the husband and wife in the same place elevated. This is accompanied by the relatives of the wife and the relatives of the husband entering amongst one another to extend the *salām*.

2) The men looking at unrelated women, some of which are uncovered and beautified, and perhaps their shins and faces are uncovered. This is not permissible. If it were not that this affair has been narrated to us and we have heard about this we would not believe that the people of *tawheed* and jealousy and protectiveness would do such a thing. And with Allāh aid is sought.

[6] *Ibn Mājah* 1532

---

6. Being lackadaisical in regard to upholding the proper etiquette of the weddings.

---

7. Going to excess regarding the wedding food.

---

8. Going to excess in regard to wedding lights.

The proof of the prohibition of going to excess has already been presented. Such as the statement of Allāh the Exalted:

﴿ وَلَا تُسْرِفُوا ۚ إِنَّهُ لَا يُحِبُّ الْمُسْرِفِينَ ﴾

But waste not by extravagance, certainly He (Allāh) likes not those who waste by extravagance.

[Sūrah al-A'rāf 7:31]

Anas ﷺ said:

مَا أَوْلَمَ النَّبِيُّ صلى الله عليه وسلم عَلَى شَيْءٍ مِنْ نِسَائِهِ، مَا أَوْلَمَ عَلَى زَيْنَبَ أَوْلَمَ بِشَاةٍ.

"The Prophet ﷺ did not give a better wedding banquet on the occasion of marrying any of his wives than the one he gave on marrying Zaynab, and that banquet consisted of one sheep."[7]

Therefore the Sunnah is to limit oneself to that which is sufficient, and to pay attention to honoring the guest without being excessive. Taking the middle course is best.

---

9. Throwing money during the wedding party; this may cause belittlement to that which has Allāh's name on it.

---

[7] *Ṣaḥīḥ al-Bukhārī* 5168

Glorifying Allāh's name and His Verses is a must whether it is on Dirham, paper money or other than that, based upon the statement of Allāh the Exalted:

﴿ وَمَن يُعَظِّمْ حُرُمَاتِ اللَّهِ فَهُوَ خَيْرٌ لَّهُ عِندَ رَبِّهِ ﴾

And whoever honors the sacred things of Allāh, then that is better for him with his Lord.

[Sūrah al-Ḥajj 22:30]

And He said:

﴿ وَمَن يُعَظِّمْ شَعَائِرَ اللَّهِ فَإِنَّهَا مِن تَقْوَى الْقُلُوبِ ﴾

And whosoever honors the Symbols of Allāh, then it is truly from the piety of the heart.

[Sūrah al-Ḥajj 22:32]

---

10. Male and female musicians attending the wedding parties or using musical tapes.

This is not permissible. Using musicians is not permissible. The proof for this from the Qur'ān, the Sunnah and the statements of the Companions has already presented for this. It is prescribed for the women to use the Daff, along with good speech and prescribed singing the night of the wedding and consummation. That which Allāh has permitted is sufficient for us to have no need of what is prohibited.

In addition to this the male and female singers received impermissible money, and those who give them the money are spending in that which is impermissible. Perhaps they give them several thousands. Thus this involved consecutive prohibitions.

---

11. The women using microphones.

The woman is commanded to lower her voice even in the affairs of legislated worship so how about for other than worship?! There is no possible excuse for women using the microphone and it is absolutely prohibited.

---

12. The women taking pictures at the wedding party.

Picture taking is prohibited in every form, and the prohibition is more severe for the women because this allows the men to see their pictures, and this occurs. And perhaps the pictures of the women will be circulated—despite the effort to safeguard against this—to groups of men, thus this will violate their honor, and an insult to their fathers and families. The established proof for the prohibition of pictures has already been presented. And the women is an *'awrah* (that which should be covered) thus the prohibited of taking her picture is more severe.

---

13. Disapproving of polygyny.

This is from the calamities presented by the enemies of the Islamic legislation, because the legislation of Islām allows polygyny. And whatever the legislation allows, we receive it with submission, compliance and acceptance. As for disapproving of the man taking two wives or more, this only comes from someone who is ignorant or those affected with the doubts thrown into their hearts by the leaders of desires from through the various means of communication. Allāh the Exalted said:

﴿ فَانكِحُوا مَا طَابَ لَكُم مِّنَ النِّسَاءِ مَثْنَىٰ وَثُلَاثَ وَرُبَاعَ ۖ فَإِنْ خِفْتُمْ أَلَّا تَعْدِلُوا فَوَاحِدَةً ﴾

> Marry women of your choice, two or three, or four but if you fear that you shall not be able to deal justly

(with them), then marry only one.

[Sūrah an-Nisā' 4:3]

The Messenger of Allāh ﷺ married more than one wife, and so did a group of his Companions.

Polygyny is permissible and allowed and it may be recommended for the man who cannot suffice with one and has a desire for polygyny.

17

Mistakes of the Tongue

---

1. Carelessness towards backbiting, tale-carrying, and mocking the Muslims regarding their appearance and manners.

This is impermissible and it is not allowed for the Muslim to be careless towards this affair. Allāh the Exalted said:

﴿ يَا أَيُّهَا الَّذِينَ آمَنُوا لَا يَسْخَرْ قَوْمٌ مِّن قَوْمٍ عَسَىٰ أَن يَكُونُوا خَيْرًا مِّنْهُمْ وَلَا نِسَاءٌ مِّن نِّسَاءٍ عَسَىٰ أَن يَكُنَّ خَيْرًا مِّنْهُنَّ ۖ وَلَا تَلْمِزُوا أَنفُسَكُمْ وَلَا تَنَابَزُوا بِالْأَلْقَابِ ۖ بِئْسَ الِاسْمُ الْفُسُوقُ بَعْدَ الْإِيمَانِ ۚ وَمَن لَّمْ يَتُبْ فَأُولَٰئِكَ هُمُ الظَّالِمُونَ ﴾

O you who believe! Let not a group scoff at another group, it may be that the latter are better than the former; nor let (some) women scoff at other women, it may be that the latter are better than the former, nor defame one another, nor insult one another by nicknames.

[Sūrah al-Ḥujurāt 49:11]

And He said in the following verse:

﴿ وَلَا يَغْتَب بَّعْضُكُم بَعْضًا ۚ أَيُحِبُّ أَحَدُكُمْ أَن يَأْكُلَ لَحْمَ أَخِيهِ مَيْتًا فَكَرِهْتُمُوهُ ﴾

And do not backbite one another. Would one of you like to eat the flesh of his dead brother? You would hate it (so hate backbiting).

[Sūrah al-Ḥujurāt 49:12]

This emphasizes that one should flee from backbiting.

As for tale-carrying, it has been narrated from Hudaifah ﷺ, that the Messenger of Allāh ﷺ said:

لاَ يَدْخُلُ الْجَنَّةَ نَمَّامٌ.

"The tale-carrier will not enter Paradise."[1]

Ibn 'Abbās ﷺ said:

أن رسول الله صلى الله عليه وسلم مر بقبرين فقال: إنهما يعذابان، وما يعذبان في كبير! بلى إنه كبير: أما أحدهما، فكان يمشي بالنميمة، وأما الآخر فكان لا يستتر من بوله.

"The Messenger of Allāh ﷺ passed by two graves. He said, 'Both of them are being punished, and they are being punished by something they did not deem to be major, but surely it is major. As for one of them, he used to carry tales; as for the other one, he did not safeguard himself from becoming soiled with his urine.'"[2]

[1] *Ṣaḥīḥ Muslim* 105

[2] Collected in *Al-Bukhārī* and *Muslim*

Tale-carrying is impermissible, and a major sin. The tale-carrier is the one who listens to the speech of the people then conveys it to those who will cause harm and division amongst the people. The tale-carrier is also the person who spreads lies to cause hatred amongst those who love each other. We ask Allāh for safety and security.

Mocking Allāh, the Qur'ān, or His Messenger is disbelief. And with Allāh refuge is sought. Allāh the Exalted said:

﴿ وَلَئِن سَأَلْتَهُمْ لَيَقُولُنَّ إِنَّمَا كُنَّا نَخُوضُ وَنَلْعَبُ ۚ قُلْ أَبِاللَّهِ وَآيَاتِهِ وَرَسُولِهِ كُنتُمْ تَسْتَهْزِئُونَ ﴿٦٥﴾ لَا تَعْتَذِرُوا قَدْ كَفَرْتُم بَعْدَ إِيمَانِكُمْ ﴿٦٦﴾ ﴾

> If you ask them (about this), they declare: "We were only talking idly and joking." Say: "Was it at Allāh, and His *ayat* and His Messenger that you were mocking?" Make no excuse; you have disbelieved after you had believed.
>
> *[Sūrah at-Tawbah 9:65-66]*

It is obligatory to love the etiquettes of the Muslims, their religion, and the guidance of their Prophet. This is proof of faith, while mocking Islām is disbelief. And with Allāh refuge is sought.

---

2. Insulting, reviling, and cursing.

All of this is prohibited. These are not from the traits of the believers. The Messenger of Allāh ﷺ said:

لَيْسَ الْمُؤْمِنُ بِالطَّعَّانِ وَلَا اللَّعَّانِ وَلَا الْفَاحِشِ وَلَا الْبَذِيءِ.

"The believer is not given to insulting, cursing a great deal, obscene talk or foul speech."[3]

---

[3] *Al-Adab al-Mufrad* 332

The Messenger of Allāh ﷺ said:

لا يَكُون اللَّعَّانُونَ شُهَدَاء وَلا شُفَعَاء يَوْمَ الْقِيَامَة.

"Those who curse a great deal will not be martyrs or intercessors on the Day of Resurrection."[4]

Likewise, the various types of insults are not permissible. The Messenger of Allāh ﷺ said:

كُلُّ اَلْمُسْلِمِ عَلَى اَلْمُسْلِمِ حَرَامٌ، دَمُهُ، وَمَالُهُ، وَعِرْضُهُ.

"All of the Muslim is inviolable upon the Muslim, his life, his wealth and his honor."[5]

And he said:

سِبَابُ الْمُسْلِمِ فُسُوقٌ.

"Insulting a Muslim is evil."[6]

And it is mentioned in the narration of Jābir bin Sulaym ﷺ that he said to the Prophet ﷺ:

اعْهَدْ إِلَيَّ. قَالَ لاَ تَسُبَّنَّ أَحَدًا. قَالَ فَمَا سَبَبْتُ بَعْدَهُ حُرًّا وَلاَ عَبْدًا وَلاَ بَعِيرًا وَلاَ شَاةً.

"Advise me." He (the Prophet) said, "Don't insult anyone." Jābir said, "After that, I never insulted a freed man, a slave, a camel, or a sheep."[7]

---

3. Making *du'ā'* against yourself, your children, or your wealth.

[4] *Ṣaḥīḥ Muslim* 2598

[5] *Ṣaḥīḥ Muslim* 2564

[6] *Ṣaḥīḥ al-Bukhārī* 7076

[7] *Sunan Abī Dāwūd* 4084

This is prohibited and not allowed. The Muslim who falls into this must train their tongue to abandon this. The Messenger of Allāh ﷺ said:

لَا تَدْعُوا عَلَى أَنْفُسِكُمْ وَلَا تَدْعُوا عَلَى أَوْلَادِكُمْ وَلَا تَدْعُوا عَلَى أَمْوَالِكُمْ لَا تُوَافِقُوا مِنَ اللَّهِ سَاعَةً يُسْأَلُ فِيهَا عَطَاءٌ فَيَسْتَجِيبُ لَكُمْ.

"Do not supplicate against yourselves, do not supplicate against your children, do not supplicate against your wealth, lest that coincide with a time when Allāh is asked and He answers your prayer."[8]

Allāh the Exalted said:

﴿ وَلَوْ يُعَجِّلُ اللَّهُ لِلنَّاسِ الشَّرَّ اسْتِعْجَالَهُم بِالْخَيْرِ لَقُضِيَ إِلَيْهِمْ أَجَلُهُمْ ﴾

And were Allāh to hasten for mankind the evil (they invoke for themselves and for their children, while in a state of anger) as He hastens for them the good (they invoke) then they would have been ruined.[9]

[Sūrah Yūnus 10:11]

---

4. Insulting days, months, and years.

The Messenger of Allāh ﷺ said:

قَالَ اللَّهُ عَزَّ وَجَلَّ يُؤْذِينِي ابْنُ آدَمَ يَسُبُّ الدَّهْرَ وَأَنَا الدَّهْرُ أُقَلِّبُ اللَّيْلَ وَالنَّهَارَ.

"Allāh the Exalted said, 'The son of Ādam inveighs against Me, he insults the time while I am Time, I alternate the night and the day.'"[10]

---

[8] *Muslim* 3014

[9] Translation by Muhsin Khan

[10] *Ṣaḥīḥ Muslim* 2246

The Messenger of Allāh ﷺ said:

لاَ يَقُولَنَّ أَحَدُكُمْ يَا خَيْبَةَ الدَّهْرِ. فَإِنَّ اللَّهَ هُوَ الدَّهْرُ.

"Let none of you say, 'O woe is the time,' for surely Allāh is the Time."[11]

His statement: "I am Time, I alternate the night and the day"; this means that which occurs from good and evil is according to the Will of Allāh and His arranging the affairs based upon His knowledge and Wisdom and no one shares with Him in these affairs. Whatever He wills will occur and what He does not will, then it will not occur. Thus it is obligatory to praise Allāh in either situation (good or evil) and to have a good thought about Allāh the Exalted and return to Him with repentance and devotion.

It is not considered insulting the time to describe years as difficult and days as evil omens as we find in the statement of Allāh the Exalted:

﴿ ثُمَّ يَأْتِي مِن بَعْدِ ذَٰلِكَ سَبْعٌ شِدَادٌ ﴾

Then will come after that, seven hard (years)

[Sūrah Yūsuf 12:48]

And His statement:

﴿ فِي يَوْمِ نَحْسٍ مُّسْتَمِرٍّ ﴾

A day of evil omen and continuous calamity

[Sūrah al-Qamar 54:19]

This is because this description is connected to the people; meaning it was difficult upon them and an evil omen for them, and the like. As for the days and years, they are not in the control of man rather all of this is by the command of Allāh.

---

[11] *Ṣaḥīḥ Muslim* 2246

5. Insulting and cursing the creations of Allāh which are not blameworthy.

This is prohibited. The Prophet ﷺ said to Jābir bin Sulaym:

لاَ تَسُبَّنَّ أَحَدًا.

"Don't insult anyone."[12]

This is general to include all the creation of Allāh. Thus this companion Jābir bin Sulaym رضي الله عنه understood his statement to be general. For this reason he said:

فَمَا سَبَبْتُ بَعْدَهُ حُرًّا وَلاَ عَبْدًا وَلاَ بَعِيرًا وَلاَ شَاةً.

"After that, I never insulted a freed man, a slave, a camel or a sheep."[13]

It has been collected by Aḥmad that:

كَانَ رَسُولُ اللَّهِ صَلَّى اللَّهُ عَلَيْهِ وَسَلَّمَ فِي سَفَرٍ، فَلَعَنَ رَجُلٌ نَاقَةً، فَقَالَ: أَيْنَ صَاحِبُ النَّاقَةِ؟ فَقَالَ الرَّجُلُ: أَنَا. فَقَالَ: أَخِّرْهَا، فَقَدْ: أُجِبْتَ فِيهَا.

"The Messenger of Allāh ﷺ was upon a journey when a man cursed him she-camel. He said, 'Where is the owner of the she-camel?' The man responded, 'I am'. He said, 'Delay her, for surely your supplication against her has been answered.'"[14]

---

[12] *Sunan Abī Dāwūd* 4084

[13] *Sunan Abī Dāwūd* 4084

[14] Collected by Aḥmad

The Prophet ﷺ forbade cursing the rooster[15], the wind[16], fleas[17] and the like. This is proof that the prohibition is general for those things where there is not a text allowing them to be criticized or cursed.

6. Insulting the Companions or the generation that followed them.

Insulting the Companions collectively is disbelief, because Allāh has praised them. He said:

﴿ مُّحَمَّدٌ رَّسُولُ اللَّهِ ۚ وَالَّذِينَ مَعَهُ أَشِدَّاءُ عَلَى الْكُفَّارِ رُحَمَاءُ بَيْنَهُمْ ۖ تَرَاهُمْ رُكَّعًا سُجَّدًا يَبْتَغُونَ فَضْلًا مِّنَ اللَّهِ وَرِضْوَانًا ۖ سِيمَاهُمْ فِي وُجُوهِهِم مِّنْ أَثَرِ السُّجُودِ ﴾

Muḥammad is the Messenger of Allāh, and those who are with him are severe against disbelievers, and merciful among themselves. You see them bowing and falling down prostrate (in prayer), seeking Bounty from Allāh and (His) Good Pleasure. The mark of them is on their faces from the traces of (their) prostration.

[Sūrah al-Fatḥ 48:29]

And the Exalted said:

[15] **Translator's note:** Zayd bin Khālid al-Juhani ﷺ said: "The Messenger of Allāh ﷺ said, 'Do not revile the rooster for it wakes you up for prayer.'" (Collected by Abū Dāwūd with an authentic chain)

[16] 'Abdullāh bin 'Abbās said, "The wind snatched away a man's cloak during the time of the Prophet ﷺ and he cursed it. The Prophet ﷺ said, 'Do not curse it, for it is under command, and if anyone curses a thing undeservedly, the curse returns upon him.'" (*Sunan Abī Dāwūd* 4908; authenticated by al-Albāni)

[17] Anas bin Malik reported that a man cursed fleas in the presence of the Prophet ﷺ, and the Prophet ﷺ said, "Do not curse them for surely a flea woke up one of the prophets for the prayer." (Collected in *Al-Adab al-Mufrad* by al-Bukhārī; al-Albāni declared it weak.)

﴿ لَّقَدْ رَضِيَ اللَّهُ عَنِ الْمُؤْمِنِينَ إِذْ يُبَايِعُونَكَ تَحْتَ الشَّجَرَةِ ﴾

Indeed, Allāh was pleased with the believers when they gave their pledge to you (O Muḥammad) under the tree.

[Sūrah al-Fatḥ 48:18]

The Prophet ﷺ said:

لاَ تَسُبُّوا أَصْحَابِي فَوَالَّذِي نَفْسِي بِيَدِهِ لَوْ أَنَّ أَحَدَكُمْ أَنْفَقَ مِثْلَ أُحُدٍ ذَهَبًا مَا أَدْرَكَ مُدَّ أَحَدِهِمْ وَلاَ نَصِيفَهُ.

"Do not revile my Companions. By Him in Whose Hand is my life, if one amongst you would have spent as much gold as Mount Uḥud it would not amount to as much as one half full spent by one of them, not even half of that."[18]

Whoever insults the Companions has rejected Allāh's praise of them, and belied the clear text of the Qur'ān; and this is disbelief. And with Allāh refuge is sought.

Insulting the Tābi'īn (the generation that followed the Companions) is evil, impermissible and a major sin, and perhaps disbelief. This is because they are the best generation after the generation of the Companions based upon the testimony of the Prophet ﷺ. And the Prophet ﷺ is the most noble and truthful of the creation. And he said:

خَيْرُ النَّاسِ قَرْنِي ثُمَّ الَّذِينَ يَلُونَهُمْ ثُمَّ الَّذِينَ يَلُونَهُمْ.

"The best people are my generation, then those that follow them, then those that follow them."[19]

---

[18] *Ṣaḥīḥ Muslim* 2540

[19] *Ṣaḥīḥ Muslim* 2533

7. Insulting and mocking the scholars.

There is no doubt that insulting them is a major sin and impermissible, and perhaps it could be disbelief and apostasy if insulting them is because of the religion of Islām and their adhering to it. And with Allāh refuge is sought from the condition of the inhabitants of the Hellfire. Allāh the Exalted said:

﴿ إِنَّمَا يَخْشَى اللَّهَ مِنْ عِبَادِهِ الْعُلَمَاءُ ﴾

It is only those who have knowledge among His slaves that fear Allāh.

[Sūrah Fāṭir 35:28]

And He said:

﴿ قُلْ هَلْ يَسْتَوِي الَّذِينَ يَعْلَمُونَ وَالَّذِينَ لَا يَعْلَمُونَ ﴾

Say: "Are those who know equal to those who know not?"

[Sūrah az-Zumar 39:9]

And Allāh the Exalted said:

﴿ شَهِدَ اللَّهُ أَنَّهُ لَا إِلَٰهَ إِلَّا هُوَ وَالْمَلَائِكَةُ وَأُولُو الْعِلْمِ قَائِمًا بِالْقِسْطِ ۚ لَا إِلَٰهَ إِلَّا هُوَ الْعَزِيزُ الْحَكِيمُ ﴾

Allāh bears witness that none has the right to be worshiped but He, and the angels, and those having knowledge (also give this witness); (He is always) maintaining His creation in Justice. None has the right to be worshiped but He, the All-Mighty, the All-Wise.

[Sūrah Āli 'Imrān 3:18]

Thus those whom Allāh has connected to Himself and the angels in testifying to *tawheed* and the truth, it is obligatory to honor them and respect them for their religion. Insulting them is to diminish them. If the insult is based upon their Islām, and their statements based upon Islām then it is clear apostasy, if he is aware of this.

Allāh the Exalted said:

﴿ وَلَئِن سَأَلْتَهُمْ لَيَقُولُنَّ إِنَّمَا كُنَّا نَخُوضُ وَنَلْعَبُ ۚ قُلْ أَبِاللَّهِ وَآيَاتِهِ وَرَسُولِهِ كُنتُمْ تَسْتَهْزِئُونَ ﴿٦٥﴾ لَا تَعْتَذِرُوا قَدْ كَفَرْتُم بَعْدَ إِيمَانِكُمْ ﴿٦٦﴾ ﴾

If you ask them (about this), they declare: "We were only talking idly and joking." Say: "Was it at Allāh, and His *ayat* and His Messenger that you were mocking?" Make no excuse; you have disbelieved after you had believed.

[Sūrah at-Tawbah 9:65-66]

18

Mistakes Related to Parties & Gatherings

1. Going to extremes concerning wedding parties, throwing food in unclean places, flaunting with the wedding parties, and other than that.

2. Using musicians and various musical instruments.

3. Throwing impermissible parties and gatherings such as New Year's Day celebrations, Mother's Day celebrations, and parties for birthdays and funerals.

4. Intermingling during the parties and displaying the beauty of women in front of men.

This is a mistake and evil, and the details have already been mentioned. Its proof can be found in various places in this treatise.

All of these affairs are widespread, may Allāh safeguard the Muslims from evils and sins and grant the insight in their religion and grant them repentance.

---

5. Eating and drinking from gold and silver vessels.

This is not permissible based upon the narration of Hudaifah ﵁. He said the Messenger of Allāh ﷺ said:

لَا تَشْرَبُوا فِي آنِيَةِ الذَّهَبِ والْفِضَّةِ، وَلَا تَأْكُلُوا فِي صِحَافِهَا.

“Do not drink from vessels made of gold or silver and do not eat from plates made of its material.”[1]

The Messenger of Allāh ﷺ said in the narration of Umm Salamah ﵂:

مَنْ شَرِبَ فِي إِنَاءٍ مِنْ ذَهَبٍ أَوْ فِضَّةٍ فَإِنَّمَا يُجَرْجِرُ فِي بَطْنِهِ نَارًا مِنْ جَهَنَّمَ.

“Whoever drinks from vessels of gold or silver, is only gulping in his stomach fire from the Hellfire.”[2]

These narrations prove the prohibition of drinking or eating from vessels of silver or gold. Included in this is every utensil made from either material such as plates, spoons, cups and everything uses to eat or drink.

---

6. Using newspaper or anything with the mention of Allāh or His Messenger on it as a table mat to eat or drink upon.

This is from the widespread evils, and from the matter which people are extremely careless about. The believer exalts the rites of Allāh and the sanctities of Allāh. As Allāh the Exalted said:

---

[1] Collected in *Al-Bukhārī* and *Muslim*

[2] *Ṣaḥīḥ Muslim* 2065

﴿ وَمَن يُعَظِّمْ شَعَائِرَ اللَّهِ فَإِنَّهَا مِن تَقْوَى الْقُلُوبِ ﴾

And whosoever honors the Symbols of Allāh, then it is truly from the piety of the heart.

[Sūrah al-Ḥajj 22:32]

And He said:

﴿ وَمَن يُعَظِّمْ حُرُمَاتِ اللَّهِ فَهُوَ خَيْرٌ لَّهُ عِندَ رَبِّهِ ﴾

And whoever honors the sacred things of Allāh, then that is better for him with his Lord.

[Sūrah al-Ḥajj 22:30]

It is incumbent to respect and honor newspapers and the like which contain the verses of Allāh and His names and to protect them from belittlement; to do so is to glorify the verses and names of Allāh. It is not permissible to belittle these papers by using them as table mats.

19

Mistakes Regarding Men's Clothing

1. Dragging the garment, robe, or pants beneath the ankles.

This is prohibited and this is something prevalent amongst the people without any fear of sin. The Messenger of Allāh ﷺ said:

مَا أَسْفَلَ مِنَ الْكَعْبَيْنِ مِنَ الإِزَارِ فَفِي النَّارِ.

"Whatever part of the lower garment is below the ankle, it is in the Fire."[1]

If the garment is worn beneath the ankle out of pride, then it is more heinous. Consequently the recompense is that Allāh will not look at this person as has been narrated by Ibn 'Umar رضي الله عنهما. The Messenger of Allāh ﷺ said:

لَا يَنْظُرُ اللَّهُ يَوْمَ الْقِيَامَةِ إِلَى مَنْ جَرَّ ثَوْبَهُ خُيَلَاءَ.

"On the Day of Judgment Allāh will not look at the man who drags his garment out of pride."[2]

---

[1] *Ṣaḥīḥ al-Bukhārī* 5787

[2] *Jāmi' at-Tirmidhī* 1730

And in the wording collected in *Ṣaḥīḥ Muslim* he said:

مَنْ جَرَّ إِزَارَهُ لَا يُرِيدُ بِذَلِكَ إِلَّا الْمَخِيلَةَ: فَإِنَّ اللَّهَ لَا يَنْظُرُ إِلَيْهِ يَوْمَ الْقِيَامَةِ.

"Whoever drags his garment only desiring arrogance, Allāh will not look at him on the Day of Judgement."[3]

Wearing the garment beneath the ankles in not permissible, and if it is done because of arrogance it is more heinous. Al Mugeerah bin Shubah ⲥ said:

رَأَيْتُ رَسُولَ اللَّهِ صَلَّى اللَّهُ عَلَيْهِ وَسَلَّمَ أَخَذَ بِرِدَاءِ سُفْيَانَ بْنِ سُهَيْلٍ وَهُوَ يَقُولُ: يَا سُفْيَانُ لَا تُسْبِلْ، فَإِنَّ اللَّهَ لَا يُحِبُّ الْمُسْبِلِينَ.

"I saw the Messenger of Allāh ⲥ grabbing the cloak of Sufyan bin Suhail while saying, 'O Sufyan do not drag your garment, for surely Allāh does not love those who drag their garments.'"[4]

---

2. Wearing tight, transparent, or flimsy clothing.

If this type of clothing reveals the *'awrah* or shows the shape of the private areas and the like, then it is obligatory to abandon it. This is based upon the statement of Allāh the Exalted:

﴿ يَا بَنِي آدَمَ قَدْ أَنزَلْنَا عَلَيْكُمْ لِبَاسًا يُوَارِي سَوْآتِكُمْ وَرِيشًا ﴾

O Children of Ādam! We have bestowed raiment
upon you to cover your private parts and as an adornment.

[Sūrah al-A'rāf 7:26]

If the clothing does not reveal the *'awrah* or describe the private areas

---

[3] *Abū Dāwūd* 4085

[4] Collected by Ibn Mājah and Ibn Hibbān.

then there is no problem wearing it even if it is tight; except if it resembles the clothing of the disbelievers, in that which is specific to them, or if it resembles women's clothing.

---

3. Wearing clothes that resemble women's clothing.

This is impermissible.

لَعَنَ رَسُولُ اللَّهِ صلى الله عليه وسلم الْمُتَشَبِّهِينَ مِنَ الرِّجَالِ بِالنِّسَاءِ، وَالْمُتَشَبِّهَاتِ مِنَ النِّسَاءِ بِالرِّجَالِ.

"The Messenger of Allāh ﷺ cursed the men who resemble women and the women who resemble men."[5]

Some of the scholars have mentioned that the meaning of "resembling" is adornments, attributes, movements and the like; not resembling them in the affairs of good.

Abū Hurayrah ﷺ said:

لَعَنَ رَسُولُ اللَّهِ صلى الله عليه وسلم الرَّجُلَ يَلْبَسُ لِبْسَةَ الْمَرْأَةِ وَالْمَرْأَةَ تَلْبَسُ لِبْسَةَ الرَّجُلِ.

"The Messenger of Allāh ﷺ cursed the man who puts on a woman's garment and the woman who puts on a man's garment."[6]

---

4. Wearing garments of fame.

These are clothes which are uncommon to that which is known to the Muslims, or that which draws attention to the person because it is very extravagant thus the person becomes famous for wearing

[5] *Ṣaḥīḥ al-Bukhārī* 5885

[6] *Sunan Abī Dāwūd* 4098

them. This also includes wearing the clothing of an ascetic, which they become known for wearing while having the ability to wear other clothing. This is prohibited. The Messenger of Allāh ﷺ said:

مَنْ لَبِسَ ثَوْبَ شُهْرَةٍ أَلْبَسَهُ اللَّهُ ثَوْبَ مَذَلَّةٍ.

"Whoever wears a garment of fame, Allāh will dress him in a garment of humiliation."[7]

Ash-Shawkani said: "This *ḥadīth* proves the prohibition of wearing clothes of fame, and that *ḥadīth* is not particular to nice clothing, rather this includes the person who wears clothing which differs from the poor so that they will be amazed by his clothing. This was the statement of Ibn Raslan. If the intent of the clothing is to be famous among the people, then there is no difference between nice clothes or shabby clothes, those clothes which are similar to the people or those clothes which differ from the people, because the prohibition is centered around becoming famous."

---

5. Wearing clothing that does not cover the *'awrah,* like sports apparel that reveals the thighs in front of the people.

The *'awrah* of the man is from the navel to the knee, thus the thigh is included in the *'awrah*. The Muslim is commanded to conceal his *'awrah* from everyone except for his wife and his right hand possession. Bahz bin Hakīm narrated from his father, from his grandfather, who said:

قلت: يا رسول الله عوراتنا ما نأتي منها وما نذر؟ قال: احفظ عورتك إلا من زوجتك، أو ما ملكت يمينك قلت: يا رسول الله، أرأيت إن كان القوم بعضهم من بعض؟ قال: إن استطعت ألا تريها أحدا فلا ترينها.

"I said, 'O Messenger of Allāh, in regard to our *'awrah*, what may we

---

[7] *Sunan Ibn Mājah*

uncover of it and what must we conceal?' He said, 'Cover your *'awrah* except from your wife and those whom your right hand possesses.' I said, 'O Messenger of Allāh, what if the people live close together?' He said, 'If you can make sure that no one sees it, then do not let anyone see it.'"[8]

The thighs are included in the *'awrah* based upon the statement of the Messenger of Allāh ﷺ:

ما بين السرة والركبة عورة.

"What is between the navel and the knee is the *'awrah*."[9]

And it has been authenticially reported that the Prophet ﷺ said:

الْفَخِذُ عَوْرَةٌ.

"The thigh is *'awrah*."[10]

Likewise, it has been authenticially reported that he command the thigh to be covered.

---

6. Being unconcerned about beautifying oneself upon going to the *masjid*.

This is in opposition to the statement of Allāh the Exalted:

﴿ يَا بَنِي آدَمَ خُذُوا زِينَتَكُمْ عِندَ كُلِّ مَسْجِدٍ ﴾

O Children of Ādam! Take your adornment while praying.

[Sūrah al-A'rāf 7:31]

[8] At-Tirmidhī 2794; Ibn Mājah 1920; classed as *hasan* by al-Albāni in *Ṣaḥīḥ at-Tirmidhī*.

[9] Collected by Aḥmad and Abū Dāwūd.

[10] *Jāmi' at-Tirmidhī*

The prayer is turning towards Allāh, and this deserves that one beautify himself for this. And the man should perfume himself, as he is able, along with removing any foul odors. This is a type of recommended beautification.

---

7. Wearing clothing that contains pictures of animate creatures, especially pictures of the disbelievers, like singers, athletes, leaders, and other famous people. Wearing garments with pictures of people, animals, or birds is prohibited.

There is a great deal of evidence showing the prohibition of picture making, hanging pictures in the home, and wearing clothing with pictures. From this proof is what has been collected in *Al-Bukhārī* and *Muslim*. Narrated from 'Ā'ishah ﵂:

عن عائشة رضي الله عنها أنها نصبت سترا وفيه تصاوير، فدخل رسول الله صلى الله عليه وسلم فنزعه، قالت: فقطعته وسادتين فكان يرتفق عليهما.

She hung up a curtain on which there were images, and the Messenger of Allāh ﷺ entered and tore it down. She said, "I cut it up and made two pillows out of it, and he used to recline upon them."[11]

The scholars have said: It is impermissible for the male and female to wear clothing containing images of animals, or to hang these images, or to use them as wallpaper. And taking these pictures is a major sin, even for curtains, ceilings, walls, beds and the like.

Wearing clothes containing pictures of the disbelievers in a form of showing amazement towards them, and befriending them; and this is a calamity. This is because the disbeliever is hated due to his disbelief, the Muslim is not amazed by him, nor does he glorify him or love him. And with Allāh help is sought.

---

[11] *Al-Bukhārī* 103 and *Muslim* 1168

8. Men wearing gold rings for fashion, wedding rings, or other than that.

It is not permissible for me to wear gold, due to the statement of the Prophet ﷺ:

أُحِلَّ الذَّهَبُ وَالْحَرِيرُ لِإِنَاثِ أُمَّتِي، وَحُرِّمَ عَلَى ذُكُورِها.

"Gold and silk have been permitted for the females of my ummah, and forbidden for the males."[12]

Al-Bara bin 'Āzib ﷺ said:

نَهَانَا عَنْ خَوَاتِيمَ أَوْ عَنْ تَخَتُّمٍ بِالذَّهَبِ.

"He forbade us from wearing rings or gold rings."[13]

Ibn 'Abbās ﷺ said:

أَنَّ رَسُولَ اللَّهِ صَلَّى اللَّه عَلَيْهِ وَسَلَّمَ رَأَى خَاتَمًا مِنْ ذَهَبٍ فِي يَدِ رَجُلٍ، فَنَزَعَهُ فَطَرَحَهُ وَقَالَ يَعْمِدُ أَحَدُكُمْ إِلَى جَمْرَةٍ مِنْ نَارٍ فَيَجْعَلُهَا فِي يَدِهِ.

"The Messenger of Allāh ﷺ saw a ring of gold in the hand of a man, so he removed it, tossed it and said, 'One of you takes a coal from the fire and puts it in his hand.'"[14]

This prohibition from wearing gold for men is general to include every purpose for wearing it. It is not permissible to wear it for beautification, engagement, or wedding rings.

---

[12] Collected by Abū Dāwūd, and by al-Hākim, who classed it as *ṣaḥīḥ*.

[13] *Ṣaḥīḥ Muslim* 2066

[14] *Ṣaḥīḥ Muslim* 2090

20

Mistakes Related to Women's Clothing

1. Wearing tight or transparent clothing which intices men to look at them.

This is from the impermissible acts. It is not permissible for a woman to wear tight clothing that reveals the sections of her body or reveals the shape of her limbs in front of non-mahram[1] men. And she cannot wear clothing which is transparent such that the color her shin can be seen. Likewise, it is not permissible for her to wear clothing which will cause men to look at her. Many women and their daugthers fall into wearing clothing like this. And if they do not repent this could perhaps be a reason for them to be punished in the fire. Allāh the Exalted said:

﴿ وَلَا يُبْدِينَ زِينَتَهُنَّ إِلَّا لِبُعُولَتِهِنَّ ﴾

And not to reveal their adornment[2] except to their

[1] **Translator's note:** The *mahram* is the husband or any other relative to whom she is prohibited to marry.

[2] **Translator's note:** Al-Baghawi رحمه الله said, "The words of Allāh the Exalted: 'And not

husbands.

[Sūrah an-Nūr 24:31]

﴿ وَلَا يَضْرِبْنَ بِأَرْجُلِهِنَّ لِيُعْلَمَ مَا يُخْفِينَ مِن زِينَتِهِنَّ ﴾

And let them not stamp their feet so as to reveal what they hide of their adornment.

[Sūrah an-Nūr 24:31]

If outwardly displaying ankle braclets is considered adornment and thus not permissible, how about displaying other types of adornment! How about the woman who reveals her waist, the size of her chest, her buttocks, or reveals her forearms, shins, and face!

There is no might or power except with Allāh, and verily from Allāh we come and to Him we shall return.

The Messenger of Allāh ﷺ said:

صِنْفَانِ مِنْ أَهْلِ النَّارِ لَمْ أَرَهُمَا قَوْمٌ مَعَهُمْ سِيَاطٌ كَأَذْنَابِ الْبَقَرِ يَضْرِبُونَ بِهَا النَّاسَ وَنِسَاءٌ كَاسِيَاتٌ عَارِيَاتٌ مُمِيلاَتٌ مَائِلاَتٌ رُءُوسُهُنَّ كَأَسْنِمَةِ الْبُخْتِ الْمَائِلَةِ لاَ يَدْخُلْنَ الْجَنَّةَ وَلاَ يَجِدْنَ رِيحَهَا وَإِنَّ رِيحَهَا لَيُوجَدُ مِنْ مَسِيرَةِ كَذَا وَكَذَا.

"There are two types of the people of Hell that I have not seen yet: men with whips like the tails of cattle, with which they strike the people, and women who are clothed yet naked, walking with an enticing gait, with something on their heads that looks like the humps of camels, leaning to one side. They will never enter Paradise or even smell its fragrance, although its fragrance can be detected from such and such

---

to show off their adornment", mean that they should not show their adornments to a non-mahram. What is meant here is the hidden adornments, as there are two kinds of adornment, hidden and apparent. Hidden adornments include anklets, henna on the foot, bracelets on the wrist, earrings and necklaces. It is not permissible for a woman to show these, or for a stranger (non-mahram man) to look at them. And what is meant by adornment is the place where the adornment is worn."

a distance."[3]

Usamah bin Zayd ﷺ said:

كساني رسول الله صلى الله عليه وسلم قبطية كثيفة فكسوتها امرأتي فقال: ما لك لم تلبس القبطية؟ قلت: كسوتها امرأتي، فقال: مرها فلتجعل تحتها غلالة، فإني أخاف أن تصف حجم عظامها.

"The Messenger of Allāh ﷺ gave me a thick Egyptian garment and I gave it to my wife to wear. He said, 'Why do I not see you wearing that Egyptian garment?' I said, 'I gave it to my wife to wear.' He said, 'Tell her to wear a gown underneath it, for I am afraid that it may describe the size of her bones.'"[4]

---

2. Wearing clothes open at the bottom which do not cover the shins and the feet, and clothes which reveal her beauty in front of non-*mahram* men.

It is not permissible for a woman to wear clothing like this in front of non-mahram men, whether they are inside her home or outside her home. It is a religious obligation upon her to have *taqwa* of Allāh and avoid wearing open clothing so she will be away from sin. And she calls towards guidance, good and chasity. The proof for this has been presented previous. May Allāh protect the daughters of the Muslims from the evil of the disbelievers and resembling them. And may He expose the plots of the hypocrites and distance us from it.

---

3. Wearing short sleeves that display the forearms in front of men in the marketplace or in the cars.

[3] *Ṣaḥīḥ Muslim* 2128

[4] Collectd by Aḥmad and al-Bayhaqi.

The Prophet ﷺ said:

الْمَرْأَةُ عَوْرَةٌ فَإِذَا خَرَجَتِ اسْتَشْرَفَهَا الشَّيْطَانُ.

"The woman is *'awrah* (that which should be covered); when she goes out, Shaytān raises the glances towards her."[5]

This means Shaytān causes the people to look at her until they fall into tribulations. And the proof prohibiting this has already been mentioned.

---

4. Wearing clothes which are particular to and resemble men's clothing.

This is prohibited. The woman has clothing which is particular to her that she is distinguished by while the man likewise has clothing particular to him by which he is distinguished from the woman. It is not permissible for the woman to resemble the man in clothing, appearance or walking.

لَعَنَ رَسُولُ اللَّهِ صَلَّى اللهُ عَلَيْهِ وَسَلَّمَ الْمُتَشَبِّهِينَ مِنَ الرِّجَالِ بِالنِّسَاءِ، وَالْمُتَشَبِّهَاتِ مِنَ النِّسَاءِ بِالرِّجَالِ.

"The Messenger of Allāh ﷺ cursed men who imitate women and women who imitate men."[6]

لَعَنَ رَسُولُ اللَّهِ صلى الله عليه وسلم الرَّجُلَ يَلْبَسُ لِبْسَةَ الْمَرْأَةِ وَالْمَرْأَةَ تَلْبَسُ لِبْسَةَ الرَّجُلِ.

"The Messenger of Allāh ﷺ cursed the man who puts on a woman's garment and the woman who puts on a man's garment."[7]

---

[5] *Jāmi' at-Tirmidhī* 1173

[6] *Al-Bukhārī* 5885

[7] *Sunan Abī Dāwūd* 4098

5. Wearing wigs because it is considered hair extensions.

Ibn 'Umar ﷺ said:

لَعَنَ النَّبِيُّ الْوَاصِلَةَ وَالْمُسْتَوْصِلَةَ وَالْوَاشِمَةَ وَالْمُسْتَوْشِمَةَ.

The Messenger of Allāh ﷺ cursed the woman who adds hair extensions and the one who has them added, the one who does tattoos and the one who has them done.[8]

Asma bint Abī Bakr ﷺ said:

جَاءَتْ امْرَأَةٌ إِلَى النَّبِيِّ صَلَّى اللَّهُ عَلَيْهِ وَسَلَّمَ فَقَالَتْ يَا رَسُولَ اللَّهِ إِنَّ لِي ابْنَةً عُرَيِّسًا أَصَابَتْهَا حَصْبَةٌ فَتَمَرَّقَ شَعْرُهَا أَفَأَصِلُهُ؟ فَقَالَ لَعَنَ اللَّهُ الْوَاصِلَةَ وَالْمُسْتَوْصِلَةَ.

"A woman came to the Prophet ﷺ and said, 'O Messenger of Allāh, I have a daughter who is newly married, and she had the measles and her hair fell out. Can I give her hair extensions?' He said, 'Allāh has cursed the one who fixes hair extensions and the one who has that done.'"[9]

It has been collected in *Al-Bukhari* and *Muslim* by Humayd bin 'Abdur-Rahman bin Awf:

أَنَّهُ سَمِعَ مُعَاوِيَةَ بْنَ أَبِي سُفْيَانَ عَامَ حَجَّ وَهُوَ عَلَى الْمِنْبَرِ وَهُوَ يَقُولُ وَتَنَاوَلَ قُصَّةً مِنْ شَعَرٍ كَانَتْ بِيَدِ حَرَسِيٍّ أَيْنَ عُلَمَاؤُكُمْ سَمِعْتُ رَسُولَ اللَّهِ صَلَّى اللَّهُ عَلَيْهِ وَسَلَّمَ يَنْهَى عَنْ مِثْلِ هَذِهِ وَيَقُولُ إِنَّمَا هَلَكَتْ بَنُو إِسْرَائِيلَ حِينَ اتَّخَذَ هَذِهِ نِسَاؤُهُمْ.

He heard Mu'āwiyah bin Abī Sufyan at the time of Ḥajj, standing on

[8] *Al-Bukhārī* 5937 and *Muslim* 2122

[9] Collected in Muslim (2122).

the *minbar* and holding a piece of hair that had been seized by his guards, saying, "Where are your scholars? I heard the Messenger of Allāh ﷺ forbidding this kind of thing and saying that Bani Isrā'eel were destroyed when their women started to use such things."

There is no doubt that wearing wigs is at the heart of this prohibition.

---

6. Using nail polish which prevents water from reaching the skin during *wuḍū'*.

It is incumbent upon the person performing *wuḍū'* to ensure water reaches all of his skin, included in this are the nails. Using nail polish prevents water from reaching all of the hand, thus the obligation of *wuḍū'* is not complete. Allāh the Exalted said:

﴿ يَا أَيُّهَا الَّذِينَ آمَنُوا إِذَا قُمْتُمْ إِلَى الصَّلَاةِ فَاغْسِلُوا وُجُوهَكُمْ وَأَيْدِيَكُمْ إِلَى الْمَرَافِقِ وَامْسَحُوا بِرُءُوسِكُمْ وَأَرْجُلَكُمْ إِلَى الْكَعْبَيْنِ ﴾

O you who believe! When you intend to offer the prayer, wash your faces and your hands up to the elbows, rub your heads, and (wash) your feet up to ankles.

[Sūrah al-Mā'idah 5:6]

If the *wuḍū'* is not complete the prayer is not correct. Which woman is pleased with her prayer not being accepted?! Therefore whoever uses nail polish must remove it before *wuḍū'*.

---

7. Wearing artificial nails or extending the fingernails and toenails.

This opposes the natural disposition. The Messenger of Allāh ﷺ said:

خَمْسٌ مِنَ الْفِطْرَةِ ـ الْخِتَانُ، وَالِاسْتِحْدَادُ، وَنَتْفُ الإِبْطِ، وَتَقْلِيمُ الأَظْفَارِ، وَقَصُّ الشَّارِبِ.

"Five things are part of the *fitrah* (natural disposition)—circumcision, shaving the pubes, plucking the armpit hairs, cutting the nails, and trimming the moustache."[10]

Anas bin Malik ﷺ said:

وُقِّتَ لَنَا فِي قَصِّ الشَّارِبِ وَتَقْلِيمِ الأَظْفَارِ وَنَتْفِ الإِبِطِ وَحَلْقِ الْعَانَةِ أَنْ لَا نَتْرُكَ أَكْثَرَ مِنْ أَرْبَعِينَ لَيْلَةً.

"He set a time for us to trim our moustaches, cut our nails, pluck our armpit hair and shave our pubic hair; we were not to leave that for more than 40 days."[11]

The women as included in what has been mentioned for the man.

[10] *Al-Bukhārī* 5889 and *Muslim* 257

[11] *Muslim* 258 and *Aḥmad* 11823

21

Imitating Non-Muslims

1. Men imitating non-Muslims by shaving the beards and growing their mustaches long.

The Prophet ﷺ commanded us to differ from the Magians and the pagans, and he ordered us to allow the beards to grow and trim the mustache. The Prophet ﷺ said:

خَالِفُوا الْمُشْرِكِينَ، وَفِّرُوا اللِّحَى، وَأَحْفُوا الشَّوَارِبَ.

"Differ from the pagans, allow the beard to grow and trim the mustache."[1]

And the Messenger of Allāh ﷺ said:

جزوا الشوارب وأرخوا اللحى خالفوا المجوس.

"Trim the mustache and let the beard grow; be different from the Magians."[2]

---

[1] *Ṣaḥīḥ al-Bukhārī* 5892

[2] *Muslim* 383

The beard is the hair that grows on the two jaws from the cheeks to the chin. This has been stated by the scholars of the Arabic language.

---

2. Men imitating non-Muslims regarding clothing.

This is prohibited based upon the *ḥadīth* of 'Abdullāh bin Amr bin Al Aws, he said:

رَأَى رَسُولُ اللَّهِ صَلَّى اللَّهُ عَلَيْهِ وَسَلَّمَ عَلَيَّ ثَوْبَيْنِ مُعَصْفَرَيْنِ فَقَالَ إِنَّ هَذِهِ مِنْ ثِيَابِ الْكُفَّارِ فَلَا تَلْبَسْهَا.

"The Messenger of Allāh ﷺ saw me wearing two garments dyed with safflower and said, 'These are garments of the disbelievers, so do not wear them.'"[3]

Abū Umamah ﵁ said, the Messenger of Allāh ﷺ said:

خَالِفُوا أَهْلَ الْكِتَابِ.

"Differ from the People of the Book."

I said:

يَا رَسُولَ اللَّهِ، إِنَّ أَهْلَ الْكِتَابِ يَتَسَرْوَلُونَ وَلَا يَأْتَزِرُونَ. فَقَالَ رَسُولُ اللَّهِ صَلَّى اللَّهُ عَلَيْهِ وَسَلَّمَ: تَسَرْوَلُوا وَائْتَزِرُوا وَخَالِفُوا أَهْلَ الْكِتَابِ.

"O Messenger of Allāh, the People of the Book wear wide pants but they do not wear waist wraps." The Messenger of Allāh ﷺ responded, "Wear wide pants and wear waist wraps and differ from the People of the Book."[4]

Every garment specific to the disbelievers should not be worn by the Muslims.

---

[3] *Muslim* 2077

[4] *Aḥmad* 21780

3. Imitating non-Muslims by celebrating non-Muslim holidays or participating with them in their celebrations.

This is impermissible. It is not permissible for the Muslim to celebrate Christian holidays or to participate with them in their celebrations. Some Muslims arrange celebrations in the institutions, businesses, and home and this allows the non-Muslims to establish the rites of their polytheistic religion. The Prophet ﷺ said:

مَنْ تَشَبَّهَ بِقَوْمٍ، فَهُوَ مِنْهُمْ.

"Whoever resembles a people is from them."[5]

Shaykhul-Islām Ibn Taymiyyah رحمه الله said, "The least of which this *ḥadīth* necessitates is the prohibition from resembling non-Muslims, although what is apparent is those who resemble them are disbelievers."

It is not permissible to participate with the People of the Book or the pagans in the holidays even by giving them the smallest gift, or congragulating them. This is to eradicate polytheism, to have a strong distinction from the people of misguidance, and it is in obedience to Allāh and His Messenger. Allāh the Exalted said:

﴿ وَلَا يَكُونُوا كَالَّذِينَ أُوتُوا الْكِتَابَ مِن قَبْلُ فَطَالَ عَلَيْهِمُ الْأَمَدُ فَقَسَتْ قُلُوبُهُمْ ۖ وَكَثِيرٌ مِّنْهُمْ فَاسِقُونَ ﴾

And let them not be like those who were given the Scripture before, and a long period passed over them, so their hearts hardened; and many of them are defiantly disobedient.

[Sūrah al-Ḥadīd 57:16]

Ibn Kathir رحمه الله said, "Allāh prohibited the believers from imitating them in anything from their foundational and subsidiary affairs."

[5] *Abū Dāwūd* 4031

4. Combing the hair over the face in imitation of the disbelievers.

This is prohibited because the Muslim is commanded to differ from the disbelievers in their general appearance and the Muslim is commanded to hold in high regard the commands of his religion and legislation. It has been authenticated in *Al-Bukhari* and *Muslim* from the *ḥadīth* of Ibn 'Abbās ﷺ that the Prophet ﷺ used to concur with the People of the Book in letting the hair hang down, then he later opposed them.[6]

This proves the intent of the legislation is to oppose them in the appearance of the hair and the manner in which they style it. This is to cut off any outward resemblance which eventually leads to inward resemblance and love towards them; and this is obvious and has been witnessed.

---

[6] **Translator's note:** The Prophet ﷺ used to like to concur with the People of the Book concerning those matters in which no command was revealed. And the People of the Book used to let their hair hang down while the pagans used to part their hair. So the Prophet ﷺ let his hair hang down, then later on he parted his hair. (*Ṣaḥīḥ al-Bukhārī* 5917)

22

Mistakes Related to Photography

1. Photographing creatures with souls without necessity.

This is from the prevalent sins which is taken so lightly it is believed to be permissible, or the people are ignorant of its prohibition. This is due to most of the Muslims having weak concern about their Hereafter and what will save them on that day.

Taking pictures of creatures with souls of any type is not permissible due to the general evidence which makes no distinction between that which has a shadow (three-dimensional) or those that are simply drawn (two-dimensional). Everything called a picture is impermissible to take or request. And the narrations proving this are numerous. From these narrations is the narration of Ibn 'Abbās رضي الله عنهما. The Prophet ﷺ said:

إِنَّ الَّذِينَ يَصْنَعُونَ هَذِهِ الصُّوَرَ يُعَذَّبُونَ يَوْمَ الْقِيَامَةِ.

"Those who make these pictures will be punished on the Day of Judgment."[1]

[1] *Ṣaḥīḥ al-Bukhārī* 5951

Other narrations concerning this have been mentioned in the 5th affair about the mistakes related to Ḥajj. Photography is not permissible except in the case of necessity, such as passports, identification and the like, from that which is necessary. And the person takes these pictures while hating it and not being pleased with it.

It is not mandatory to pursue the pictures on the can, cartons, newspapers and the like, because they are insignificant, and too numerous. There is an Islamic jurisprudence principle which states 'hardship grants a concession for ease'.

---

2. Hanging pictures in sitting rooms of creatures with souls.

This is worst than taking the photograph because this is a pathway which leads to exalting it. Narrated from 'Ā'ishah ﷺ:

عن عائشة رضي الله عنها أنها نصبت سترا وفيه تصاوير، فدخل رسول الله صلى الله عليه وسلم فنزعه.

She hung up a curtain on which there were images, and the Messenger of Allāh ﷺ entered and tore it down.[2]

'Alī bin Abī Tālib said that the Prophet ﷺ ordered that no image be left without defacing it.[3]

Thus hanging pictures is obvious sin, and if it is a stereoscopic image, or three dimensional image, the affairs is more severe. It is obligatory upon the Muslim to fear Allāh, and remove, and break the three dimensional images in their homes and remove the pictures of creatures with souls whether it be humans, animals, birds or the like.

May Allāh protect us from the evil of sin. And with Allāh aid is sought.

---

[2] *Al-Bukhārī* 103 and *Muslim* 1168

[3] *Muslim* 969

---

3. Saving pictures of creatures with souls for the purpose of reminiscing .

Saving pictures for reminiscing is not allowed and not permissible because the Muslim is commanded to deface images and break statues, thus it is not allowed to save them. The narrations containing the command to remove and deface images have been mentioned, thus this is a command and action of the Prophet ﷺ.

---

4. Buying photography devices for those who will use it for impermissible matters.

It is obligatory to distance oneself from this because the Prophet ﷺ said:

إِنَّ اللّه إِذَا حَرَّمَ شَيْئاً حَرَّمَ ثَمَنَهُ.

"When Allāh forbids a thing, He (also) forbids its price."[4]

In another *ḥadīth* he forbade the money earned from selling statues and idols. The scholars past and present have stated that selling pictures and images is not permissible, and the money earned from it is likewise impermissible. There is no doubt that the equipment for photography carries the same ruling as the ruling the Prophet ﷺ gave for devices that produce alcohol; that they should be broken.

---

[4] *Abū Dāwūd* 3488; classed as *ṣaḥīḥ* by Shaykh al-Albāni in *Ghāyat al-Marām* (318).

23

Mistakes Regarding Family

1. The absence of unity among the spouses, anger in the home for the slightest reason, and apathy towards treating the wives kindly.

It is a must that the husband is patient with the shortcomings of his wife, and the wife should likewise be patient, and they should avoid getting angry. This was from the advice of the Prophet ﷺ:

لاَ تَغْضَبْ.

"Don't become angry."[1]

If one spouse becomes angry it is recommended that the other one is patient and does not respond to anger with anger, so Shaytān does not enter into the situation.

It is upon the man to live with his wife in kindness. Allāh the Exalted said:

﴿ وَعَاشِرُوهُنَّ بِالْمَعْرُوفِ ﴾

[1] *Ṣaḥīḥ al-Bukhārī* 6116

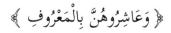

Live with them in kindness and equity.

[Sūrah an Nisā 4:19]

The Prophet ﷺ said:

اسْتَوْصُوا بِالنِّسَاءِ خَيْرًا.

"Act kindly towards the women."[2]

And in another narration he said:

أَكْمَلُ الْمُؤْمِنِينَ إِيمَانًا أَحْسَنُهُمْ خُلُقًا وَخِيَارُكُمْ خِيَارُكُمْ لِنِسَائِهِمْ خُلُقًا.

"The most complete believer in faith are those with the best character and the best of you are the best of you towards your wives in manners."[3]

It is upon the wife to treat her husband kindly and obey him in what he commands her as long as it is not disobedience. She should not leave his home unless he is pleased with it. Paradise is hers if she is truthful towards him and obeys him. The Prophet ﷺ said:

أيما امرأة ماتت، وزوجها عنها راضٍ دخلت الجنة.

"Any woman who dies while her husband is pleased with her will enter Paradise."[4]

The man is the maintainer and protector of the woman as Allāh the Exalted said:

﴿ الرِّجَالُ قَوَّامُونَ عَلَى النِّسَاءِ بِمَا فَضَّلَ اللَّهُ بَعْضَهُمْ عَلَىٰ بَعْضٍ ﴾

Men are the protectors and maintainers of women,

---

[2] *Ṣaḥīḥ Muslim* 1468

[3] Collected by at-Tirmidhī and Aḥmad.

[4] Collected by at-Tirmidhī and Ibn Mājah.

because Allāh has made one of them to excel the other

[Sūrah an-Nisā' 4:34]

And He said:

﴿ وَلِلرِّجَالِ عَلَيْهِنَّ دَرَجَةٌ ۗ وَاللَّهُ عَزِيزٌ حَكِيمٌ ﴾

But men have a degree (of responsibility) over them. And Allāh is All-Mighty, All-Wise.

[Sūrah al-Baqarah 2:228]

The Messenger of Allāh ﷺ said:

إذا صلت المرأة خمسها و صامت شهرها و حصنت فرجها و أطاعت زوجها قيل لها: ادخلي الجنة من أي أبواب الجنة شئت.

"If a woman prays her five (daily prayers), fasts her month (Ramaḍān), guards her chastity and obeys her husband, it will be said to her: 'Enter Paradise from whichever of the gates of Paradise you wish.'"[5]

---

2. Injustice among the children in regard to spending and giving.

Justice between the children is obligatory due to the statement of the Prophet ﷺ:

فَاتَّقُوا اللَّهَ وَاعْدِلُوا بَيْنَ أَوْلَادِكُمْ.

"Fear Allāh and treat your children fairly."[6]

Nu'man bin Bashir رضي الله عنه said:

أَنَّ أَبَاهُ أَتَى بِهِ إِلَى رَسُولِ اللَّهِ صَلَّى اللَّهُ عَلَيْهِ وَسَلَّمَ فَقَالَ: إِنِّي نَحَلْتُ ابْنِي

[5] From the *ḥadīth* of Abū Hurayrah; collected by Ibn Hibbān and classed as *ṣaḥīḥ* by al-Albāni in *Ṣaḥīḥ al-Jāmi'* (660).

[6] *Al-Bukhārī* 2587

هَذَا غُلَامًا، فَقَالَ: أَكُلَّ وَلَدِكَ نَحَلْتَ مِثْلَهُ؟ قَالَ لَا قَالَ فَارْجِعْهُ.

"His father brought him to the Messenger of Allāh ﷺ and said, 'I have given a slave to this son of mine.' He said, 'Have you given a similar gift to all your children?' He said, 'No.' He said, 'Then return him.'"[7]

But if one of the children has a legislated reason to receive something, for example he works for his father, then this is his right. Likewise if the child is given a something for the purpose of marriage it is not obligatory to give something similar to the other children. But if the child has done a similar act which causes the parent to give something to the other children, then it is obligatory to give it to him as well. And Allāh knows best.

---

3. Injustice regarding allotment between wives.

Allotment is of two types, wealth and body.

As for the body, it is to give the wife her night similar to her co-wife. It must be fair among all of them, and it is impermissible to be unjust in this matter. Giving the wives equal personal time is obligatory. The proof that it is obligatory is the statement of Allāh the Exalted:

﴿ وَلَا يَجْرِمَنَّكُمْ شَنَآنُ قَوْمٍ عَلَىٰٓ أَلَّا تَعْدِلُوا ۚ اعْدِلُوا هُوَ أَقْرَبُ لِلتَّقْوَىٰ ﴾

And let not the enmity and hatred of others make you avoid justice. Be just: that is nearer to piety.

[Sūrah al-Mā'idah 5:8]

From the ways this is implemented can be found in the statement of Anas ﷺ:

مِنَ السُّنَّةِ إِذَا تَزَوَّجَ الرَّجُلُ البِكْرَ عَلَى الثَّيِّبِ أَقَامَ عِنْدَهَا سَبْعًا وَقَسَمَ، وَإِذَا

---

[7] *Al-Bukhārī* 2586 and *Muslim* 162

تَزَوَّجَ الثَّيِّبَ عَلَى الْبِكْرِ أَقَامَ عِنْدَهَا ثَلاَثًا ثُمَّ قَسَمَ.

"The Sunnah when a man marries a virgin after he already has a wife, is that he stays with her seven (nights) and then by turns. And when he married a previously married woman when he already has a wife, he stays with her three (nights) and then by turns."[8]

Whoever is unjust has fallen into sin. The Prophet ﷺ said:

مَنْ كَانَ لَهُ امْرَأَتَانِ يَمِيلُ لإِحْدَاهُمَا عَلَى الأُخْرَى جَاءَ يَوْمَ الْقِيَامَةِ أَحَدُ شِقَّيْهِ مَائِلٌ.

"Whoever has two wives and is inclined to favor one of them over the other, he will come on the Day of Resurrection with half of his body leaning."[9]

It is also obligatory upon the husband to be fair between his wives as it relates to finance and it is not permissible to be unjust in this matter.

---

4. Not showing concern for marrying religious individuals with good character.

Allāh the Exalted said:

﴿ وَأَنكِحُوا الْأَيَامَىٰ مِنكُمْ وَالصَّالِحِينَ مِنْ عِبَادِكُمْ وَإِمَائِكُمْ ۚ إِن يَكُونُوا فُقَرَاءَ يُغْنِهِمُ اللَّهُ مِن فَضْلِهِ ﴾

And marry those among you who are single and (also marry) the pious, of your (male) slaves and maid-servants. If they be poor, Allāh will enrich them out of His Bounty.

[Sūrah an-Nūr 24:32]

---

[8] *Ṣaḥīḥ al-Bukhārī* 5214

[9] *Sunan an-Nasā'ī* 3942

The Prophet ﷺ said:

إِذَا أَتَاكُمْ مَنْ تَرْضَوْنَ دِينَهُ وَخُلُقَهُ فَزَوِّجُوهُ إِلَّا تَفْعَلُوا تَكُنْ فِتْنَةٌ فِي الْأَرْضِ وَفَسَادٌ عَرِيضٌ.

"If there comes to you one who pleases you with his religion and his manners, then marry him; if you do not do so there will be corruption in the land and widespread evil."[10]

---

5. Being careless in regard to shaking hands of the opposite sex among non-mahrams.

This is impermissible, because the woman is not allowed to display her hand to be seen so how can she do so to be touched?! The Prophet ﷺ said:

الْمَرْأَةُ عَوْرَةٌ.

"The woman is *'awrah.*"[11]

And the Messenger of Allāh ﷺ said:

لَأَنْ يُطْعَنَ فِي رَأْسِ أَحَدِكُمْ بِمِخْيَطٍ مِنْ حَدِيدٍ، خَيْرٌ لَهُ مِنْ أَنْ يَمَسَّ امْرَأَةً لَا تَحِلُّ لَهُ.

"For one of you to be stabbed in the head with an iron pick is better for him than that he should touch a woman who is not permissible for him."[12]

Prophet Muḥammad ﷺ was our example and he did not shake the hands of women. 'Ā'ishah ﵂ said:

---

[10] Collected by at-Tirmidhī (1085).

[11] *Jāmi' at-Tirmidhī* 1173

[12] Collected in at-Tabarani in *Al-Kabeer* (486); Shaykh al-Albāni said in *Ṣaḥīḥ al-Jāmi'* (5045) that this *ḥadīth* is *ṣaḥīḥ*.

والله ما مسَّتْ يـدُهُ يـدَ امرأةٍ قطُّ في المبايعة.

"I swear by Allāh, his hand never touched the hand of a woman during the oath of allegiance."[13]

---

6. The woman being careless about wearing *ḥijāb* around the husband's brothers, cousins and other non-mahram men.

This is from the prevalent evils. The woman is commanded with *ḥijāb* and to cover her face around all non-mahram men. If the non-mahram men are relatives of the husband such as his brothers, and cousins the affairs is more severe. The Prophet ﷺ said:

إِيَّاكُمْ وَالدُّخُولَ عَلَى النِّسَاءِ فَقَالَ رَجُلٌ مِنْ الْأَنْصَارِ يَا رَسُولَ اللَّهِ أَفَرَأَيْتَ الْحَمْوَ قَالَ الْحَمْوُ الْمَوْتُ.

"Beware of entering upon women. A man from among the Anṣār said, 'O Messenger of Allāh, what about the in-laws?' He said, 'The in-law is death.'"[14]

The in-laws for the wife are the close relatives of the husband (his brother) this is because this close relative is from the last person about whom as suspicion would arise.

---

7. The men being careless about being alone with women in homes and cars.

It is not permissible for a man to be alone with a woman or for a woman to be alone with a man unless they are from their close relatives whom they can never marry. They cannot be alone together in the home, a car, or anywhere else. The Prophet ﷺ said:

---

[13] *Muslim* 1866

[14] *Al-Bukhārī* 4934 and *Muslim* 2172

لَا يَخْلُوَنَّ رَجُلٌ بِامْرَأَةٍ إِلَّا وَمَعَهَا ذُو مَحْرَمٍ.

"No one of you should be alone with a woman unless a *mahram* is present."[15]

And the Prophet ﷺ said:

لَا يَخْلُوَنَّ رَجُلٌ بِامْرَأَةٍ فَإِنَّ ثَالِثَهُمَا الشَّيْطَانَ.

"Let no man be alone with a woman for surely the Shaytān is the third one present."[16]

The seclusion which is impermissible is when the door of the room, home or car is closed, or when they are hidden from the eyes of the people. This is the seclusion which is not allowed. These are the guidelines mentioned by the scholars.

---

8. Using butlers, maids, and drivers without an urgent need to do so.

If the drivers and maids are married and Muslim; this less of a harm and allowable. In some cases you find young unmarried maids who have desires and consequently evil occurs. Those who know the condition of the homes and the condition of the drivers and maids, also know that many people fall into sin and evil without realizing it. Very few people stress restrictions in regard to the maids, and order them with covering and modesty and remaining in the home. Whoever desires to safeguard his religion, from those individuals who hire maids and drivers, then implement the commands of the religion upon them. Protect your home, yourself and your children from the deviations of the drivers, and uncovering of the maids. And with Allāh help is sought.

---

[15] Collected in *Al-Bukhārī* and *Muslim.*

[16] Collected in *Al-Bukhārī* and *Muslim.*

9. Butlers mixing with the women and maids mixing with the men.

There is no doubt that men and women being alone is impermissible, and this includes the butler. The head of household is responsible for this and for the apathy towards it. Some of the homes allow the people to be alone with the drivers, maids and butler; and this is not permissible. The man and woman responsible for the home are sinning if they do not disapprove of this. It is a must to mean the necessary means to prevent mixing and seclusion which will bring about impermissible acts and lewdness. May Allāh grant the Muslims insight and repel from them the means to sin and transgression.

10. Not using close relatives as drivers if the need arises.

This is a clear mistake. That is because it is not permissible for the woman to travel without a *mahram*, even for the purpose of Ḥajj, so how about for other than Ḥajj?! This is based upon the statement of the Prophet ﷺ:

لاَ يَحِلُّ لِامْرَأَةٍ تُؤْمِنُ بِاللَّهِ وَالْيَوْمِ الآخِرِ تُسَافِرُ مَسِيرَةَ يَوْمٍ وَلَيْلَةٍ إِلاَّ مَعَ ذِي مَحْرَمٍ عَلَيْهَا.

"It is not permissible for a woman who believes in Allāh and the Last Day to make a journey of one day and night unless she is accompanied by a *mahram*."[17]

11. The woman traveling by land, sea, or air without a *mahram*.

This is not permissible and the evidence has already been mentioned.

[17] *Ṣaḥīḥ Muslim* 1339

12. Carelessness in regard to hiring non-Muslims.

If this occurs in the Arabian Peninsula it is impermissible due to the statement of the Prophet ﷺ:

لَا يَجْتَمِعُ دِينَانِ فِي جَزِيرَةِ الْعَرَبِ أخرجوا اليهود والنصارى من جزيرة العرب.

"Two religions should not unite in the Arabian Peninsula; remove the Jews and Christians from the Arabian Peninsula."[18]

Hiring non-Muslims for work or housekeeping services brings about a great deal of evil, such as them importing their religious habits, and vile manners. Thus when they remain in a society it will have an effect upon its people. And there are narrations which mention the harms as a result of non-Muslims mixing with Muslims.

[18] Collected in *Al-Bukhārī.*

24

Mistakes Regarding the Home

1. Going to the extreme regarding furniture.

This is in opposition to the command to be moderate in this affair, and avoid being excessive. Allāh the Exalted said:

﴿ وَلَا تُسْرِفُوا ۚ إِنَّهُ لَا يُحِبُّ الْمُسْرِفِينَ ﴾

But waste not by extravagance, certainly He (Allāh) likes not those who waste by extravagance.

[Sūrah al-A'rāf 7:31]

And He said:

﴿ وَلَا تُبَذِّرْ تَبْذِيرًا ﴾

But do not spend wastefully.

[Sūrah al-Isrā' 17:26]

Likewise flaunting and showing off by overburdening oneself by purchasing furniture above their means; the believer has been prohibited from this because the intent is evil. But there is nothing wrong with furnishing and dressing up the home if it is done without extravagance and excess such as decorating the walls with prayer rugs, and using impermissible material such as silk and the like. And buying the most expensive furniture possible is from extravagance and excess. Balance is better in regards to everything, and everyone does in accordance to his means. And whoever takes the Salaf and their lives as an example, this is more complete.

---

2. Some of the homes exposing others.

This must be warned against. The homes are *'awrah* and it is from the rights of the home that its secrets are protected and safeguarded. Exposing secrets of the home to outsiders will cause harm to the woman and man of the household. And there matters are better concealed and treated.

25

Mistakes Regarding Food & Drink

1. Overindulgence regarding food and drink, wasting food, and throwing food into filthy places.

Allāh the Exalted said:

﴿ وَكُلُوا وَاشْرَبُوا وَلَا تُسْرِفُوا ۚ إِنَّهُ لَا يُحِبُّ الْمُسْرِفِينَ ﴾

Eat and drink but waste not by extravagance, certainly He (Allāh) likes not those who waste by extravagance.

[Sūrah al-A'rāf 7:31]

And the Exalted said:

﴿ وَلَا تُبَذِّرْ تَبْذِيرًا ﴿٢٦﴾ إِنَّ الْمُبَذِّرِينَ كَانُوا إِخْوَانَ الشَّيَاطِينِ ۖ وَكَانَ الشَّيْطَانُ لِرَبِّهِ كَفُورًا ﴿٢٧﴾ ﴾

But spend not wastefully (your wealth) in the manner of a spendthrift. Verily, spendthrifts are brothers of the devils, and the devil is ever ungrateful to his Lord.

[Sūrah al-Isrā' 17:26-27]

Extravagance is spending beyond the known limit to honor the guest. If this food will be eaten or given in charity this is good. But if the destination of this food is the garbage can or an unclean place; then this is to belittle the favor of Allāh and utilizing the favors in a manner He is not pleased with. Especially when so many people are hungry, thus it is feared that the extravagant person when bring upon himself the punishment.

The Messenger of Allāh ﷺ said:

كُلُوا وَاشْرَبُوا وَتَصَدَّقُوا وَالْبَسُوا مَا لَمْ يُخَالِطْهُ إِسْرَافٌ أَوْ مَخِيلَةٌ.

"Eat and drink, give charity and wear clothes, as long as that does not involve any extravagance or arrogance."[1]

---

2. Eating and drinking with the left hand.

This is prohibited because it resembles the manner in which Shaytān eats. The Messenger of Allāh ﷺ said:

إِذَا أَكَلَ أَحَدُكُمْ فَلْيَأْكُلْ بِيَمِينِهِ، وَإِذَا شَرِبَ فَلْيَشْرَبْ بِيَمِينِهِ، فَإِنَّ الشَّيْطَانَ يَأْكُلُ بِشِمَالِهِ، وَيَشْرَبُ بِشِمَالِهِ.

"When one of you eats, let him eat with his right hand, and when he drinks let him drink with his right hand, because the devil eats and drinks with his left hand."[2]

---

3. Being careless about throwing leftover food down the drain.

My grandfather, the previous mufti of Saudi Arabia, Shaykh Muḥammad bin Ibrāhīm, was asked about this, and answered: "Allāh has blessed His slaves with various favors, and commanded them to

---

[1] An Nasi'i 2559

[2] Muslim 1911

show gratitude. From these favors is the favor of food and drink. The Exalted said:

$$\{ \text{كُلُوا مِن رِّزْقِ رَبِّكُمْ وَاشْكُرُوا لَهُ} \}$$

"Eat of the provision of your Lord, and be grateful to Him."

[*Sūrah Saba' 34:15*]

"Thus, it is obligatory upon the slave to show gratitude for this favor. And from gratitude is to not belittle it or throw it in filthy places. As for washing the hands in the sink after eating, this requires details. If there remains some food on his hand which he intends to throw down the drain then this is not permissible, because this is belittle the favor and not honoring it. But if there only remains some remnants connected to his hand or the utensil without any food portions, bread crumbs or the like, then there is no problem with washing it in any place his chooses, because what remains is only the unclean portion of food that has no value, and no one would desire to eat this; rather it is only that which makes his hands dirty and sticky. Even if the like of this was gather together in a vessel it would not be desirable regardless of how hungry or thirsty the person was. The same applies if it is accompanied by something small which is difficult to preserve such as grains of rice and the like."

With this, we know that pouring liquid food, or drinks which people can benefit from or desire to drink, is prohibited, because it is considered belittlement of the favor.

---

4. Not mentioning the name of Allāh when eating or drinking.

We are commanded to mention the name of Allāh before eating and drinking. This is based upon the *ḥadīth* of 'Umar bin Abī Salamah 🙏. The Prophet ﷺ said to him:

$$\text{يَا غُلاَمُ سَمِّ اللَّهَ، وَكُلْ بِيَمِينِكَ وَكُلْ مِمَّا يَلِيكَ.}$$

"O young boy, mention the name of Allāh, eat with your right hand, and eat what is close to you."[3]

The Prophet ﷺ said:

إِنَّ الشَّيْطَانَ يَسْتَحِلُّ الطَّعَامَ أَنْ لاَ يُذْكَرَ اسْمُ اللَّهِ عَلَيْهِ.

"Verily Shaytān deems as permissible the food in which the name of Allāh is not mentioned over."[4]

This is a summary of the narration; there is a story that goes along with it.

---

[3] *Ṣaḥīḥ al-Bukhārī* 5376 ('Umar bin Abī Salamah said, "I was a boy under the care of Allāh's Messenger ﷺ and my hand used to go around the dish while I was eating. So Allāh's Messenger ﷺ said to me, 'O young boy! Mention the name of Allāh and eat with your right hand, and eat of the dish what is nearer to you.' Since then I have applied those instructions when eating.")

[4] *Muslim* 2017

26

Mistakes Related to Funerals

1. Reciters attending gatherings for condolences.

This is a newly invented innovation which has nothing to do with the religion; believing that it is a legislated act of worship is surely an affair which Allāh has sent no authority for. Allāh the Exalted said:

﴿ أَمْ لَهُمْ شُرَكَاءُ شَرَعُوا لَهُم مِّنَ الدِّينِ مَا لَمْ يَأْذَن بِهِ اللَّهُ ﴾

Or have they partners with Allāh (false gods), who have instituted for them a religion which Allāh has not allowed.

[Sūrah ash-Shūrā 42:21]

This is a newly invented matter. This is a practice where the reciters attend during the days of condolences. This is not from the guidance of the Prophet ﷺ, and this was not done by any of the virtuous generations.

Sitting for condolences in principle is hated; rather it is the Sunnah for everyone to get on about their work so the sadness will dissipate. As for the people gathering to receive condolences the scholars of the *madhāhib* which are followed have stated this is hated. Thus if sitting to receive condolences is hated, there is no doubt that the newly invented matters such as hiring reciters and the burden is cost to do so is an evil innovation.

Ibn al-Qayyim ﷺ said in *Al-Hady*: "It was from the guidance of the Prophet ﷺ to give condolences to the family of the deceased, but it was not from his guidance to gather for condolences and recite the Qur'ān; not at the grave site or any other place. All of this is a hated newly invented innovation."

---

2. The family of the deceased holding a feast for the visitors.

This is in contrast to the Sunnah, and it busies the family of the deceased. The Sunnah is that enough food should be prepared for the family of the deceased to suffice them. This is based upon the narration of 'Abdullāh bin Ja'far ﷺ when condolences were given to the family of Ja'far when Ja'far was killed. The Messenger of Allāh ﷺ said:

اصْنَعُوا لِآلِ جَعْفَرٍ طَعَامًا، فَقَدْ أَتَاهُمْ مَا يَشْغَلُهُمْ.

"Prepare food for the family of Ja'far, for there has befallen them that which has preoccupied them."[1]

Ibn al-Qayyim ﷺ said: "It was from the guidance of the Prophet ﷺ that the family of the decease was not burdened with preparing food for the people, rather he commanded the people prepare food and send to them. And this is from the greatest displays of noble manners, good practices and removing a burden from the family because there calamity has preoccupied them from feeding the people."

---

[1] *Sunan Ibn Mājah*

3. Throwing a party for the visitors, placing lights in the home, and giving gifts.

This is an innovation. Placing lights at the home of the deceased is akin to a death announcement, and this is prohibited. It has been mentioned in the second affair, that it is the Sunnah to assist the family by giving them food, and to not burden them with things which Allāh has not sent down any authorization for. The Sunnah is best and it is blessed, while innovation is evil and a calamity.

4. Wailing over the dead.

This is impermissible. This is from the traits of the Pre-Islamic Days of Ignorance, and from the braces of disbelief. The Messenger of Allāh ﷺ said:

اثْنَتَانِ فِي النَّاسِ هُمَا بِهِمْ كُفْرٌ الطَّعْنُ فِي النَّسَبِ وَالنِّيَاحَةُ عَلَى الْمَيِّتِ.

"There are two qualities that exist among people which are qualities of disbelief: slandering people's lineage and wailing over the dead."[2]

And the Messenger of Allāh ﷺ said:

أَرْبَعٌ فِي أُمَّتِي مِنْ أَمْرِ الْجَاهِلِيَّةِ لا يَتْرُكُونَهُنَّ: الْفَخْرُ فِي الأَحْسَابِ، وَالطَّعْنُ فِي الأَنْسَابِ، وَالاسْتِسْقَاءُ بِالنُّجُومِ، وَالنِّيَاحَةُ.

"There are four matters within my *ummah* from the affairs of the Pre-Islamic Days of Ignorance which they will not abandon: Bragging of noble descent, slandering people's lineage, seeking rain from the stars, and wailing of the dead."[3]

And he said:

[2] *Ṣaḥīḥ Muslim* 67

[3] *Ṣaḥīḥ Muslim* 934

النَّائِحَةُ إِذَا لَمْ تَتُبْ قَبْلَ مَوْتِهَا تُقَامُ يَوْمَ الْقِيَامَةِ وَعَلَيْهَا سِرْبَالٌ مِنْ قَطِرَانٍ وَدِرْعٌ مِنْ جَرَبٍ.

"If the hired wailing woman does not repent before she dies, she will be made to stand on the Day of Resurrection wearing a garment of tar and shield of scabs."[4]

Umm Salamah ﵂ said:

لَمَّا مَاتَ أَبُو سَلَمَةَ قُلْتُ غَرِيبٌ وَفِي أَرْضِ غُرْبَةٍ لأَبْكِيَنَّهُ بُكَاءً يُتَحَدَّثُ عَنْهُ. فَكُنْتُ قَدْ تَهَيَّأْتُ لِلْبُكَاءِ عَلَيْهِ إِذْ أَقْبَلَتِ امْرَأَةٌ مِنَ الصَّعِيدِ تُرِيدُ أَنْ تُسْعِدَنِي فَاسْتَقْبَلَهَا رَسُولُ اللَّهِ صلى الله عليه وسلم وَقَالَ أَتُرِيدِينَ أَنْ تُدْخِلِي الشَّيْطَانَ بَيْتًا أَخْرَجَهُ اللَّهُ مِنْهُ. فَكَفَفْتُ عَنِ الْبُكَاءِ فَلَمْ أَبْكِ.

"When Abū Salamah died I said, 'I am a stranger in a strange land; I shall weep for him in a manner that would be talked of.' I made preparation for weeping for him when a woman from the upper side of the city came there who intended to help me (in weeping). She happened to come across the Messenger of Allāh ﷺ and he said, 'Do you intend to bring Shaytān into a house from which Allāh has driven him out?' I (Umm Salamah), therefore, refrained from weeping and I did not weep."[5]

Wailing is to raise the voice with sobbing over the deceased, and crying with a loud elevated voice which resembles coo of a pigeon. All of this is to hate the decree of Allāh and that negates the obligatory patience. This is from the major sins due to the severe threat and punishment which accompanies it.

---

[4] *Ṣaḥīḥ Muslim* 934

[5] *Ṣaḥīḥ Muslim* 922

5. Striking the cheeks, tearing the garment, and crying with the cry from the Pre-Islamic Days of Ignorance.

These actions are evil and impermissible, because these actions are traits from the Pre-Islamic Days of Ignorance, and it is proof the individual is not pleased with the decree of Allāh, and they were not patient with the calamity. The Messenger of Allāh ﷺ said:

لَيْسَ مِنَّا مَنْ لَطَمَ الْخُدُودَ وَشَقَّ الْجُيُوبَ وَدَعَا بِدَعْوَى الْجَاهِلِيَّةِ.

"They are not from us, those who strike their cheeks, tear their garment, or cries with the cry of the Pre-Islamic Days of Ignorance."[6]

"They are not from us" means they are not from the people of our Sunnah or our way. This statement proves these actions are prohibited.

Abū Burda bin Abū Musa said:

وَجِعَ أَبُو مُوسَى وَجَعًا فَغُشِيَ عَلَيْهِ وَرَأْسُهُ فِي حَجْرِ امْرَأَةٍ مِنْ أَهْلِهِ فَصَاحَتِ امْرَأَةٌ مِنْ أَهْلِهِ فَلَمْ يَسْتَطِعْ أَنْ يَرُدَّ عَلَيْهَا شَيْئًا فَلَمَّا أَفَاقَ قَالَ أَنَا بَرِيءٌ مِمَّا بَرِئَ مِنْهُ رَسُولُ اللَّهِ صلى الله عليه وسلم فَإِنَّ رَسُولَ اللَّهِ صلى الله عليه وسلم بَرِئَ مِنَ الصَّالِقَةِ وَالْحَالِقَةِ وَالشَّاقَّةِ.

"Abū Musa was afflicted with grave pain and he became unconscious and his head was in the lap of a lady of his household. One of the women of his household wailed. He (Abū Musa) was unable (because of weakness) to say anything to her. But when he recovered he said: I am free from the one whom the Messenger of Allāh ﷺ is free from. Verily, the Messenger of Allāh ﷺ is free from the woman who wails loudly, shaves her hair and tears (her garment in grief)."[7]

[6] *Al-Bukhārī* 1294 and *Muslim* 103

[7] *Ṣaḥīḥ Muslim* 104

---

6. Women following the funeral procession.

This is prohibited based upon the *ḥadīth* of Umm Attiya رضي الله عنها. She said:

كُنَّا نُنْهَى عَنِ اتِّبَاعِ الجَنَائِزِ وَلَمْ يُعْزَمْ عَلَيْنَا.

"We were forbidden to follow funeral processions, but not strictly."[8]

Women following funeral processions is a means which leads to evil matters, causes them to wail, and results in an absence of patience and being pleased.

---

7. Mourning the deceased for more than three days except in the case of the wife—she is allowed to mourn her husband for four months and ten days.

This is impermissible and not allowed. Umm Habībah رضي الله عنها said, "I heard the Messenger of Allāh ﷺ say on the *minbar*:

لاَ يَحِلُّ لِامْرَأَةٍ تُؤْمِنُ بِاللَّهِ وَالْيَوْمِ الآخِرِ تَحِدُّ عَلَى مَيِّتٍ فَوْقَ ثَلاَثٍ إِلاَّ عَلَى زَوْجٍ فَإِنَّهَا تَحِدُّ عَلَيْهِ أَرْبَعَةَ أَشْهُرٍ وَعَشْرًا.

"It is not permissible for a woman who believes in Allāh and the Last Day to mourn for anyone who dies for more than three days except for a husband; she should mourn for him for four months and ten (days)."[9]

The intended meaning of "mourning" here is when she leaves off beautifying herself, using perfume, dye, and the like. These are from the matters prohibited for the woman. Thus she cannot mourn for anyone more than three days with the exception of her husband. Allāh the Exalted said:

---

[8] *Al-Bukhārī* 1219; *Ṣaḥīḥ Muslim* 938

[9] *Sunan an-Nasā'ī* 3503

﴿ وَالَّذِينَ يُتَوَفَّوْنَ مِنكُمْ وَيَذَرُونَ أَزْوَاجًا يَتَرَبَّصْنَ بِأَنفُسِهِنَّ أَرْبَعَةَ أَشْهُرٍ وَعَشْرًا ﴾

And those of you who die and leave wives behind them, they (the wives) shall wait for four months and ten days.

[Sūrah al-Baqarah 2:234]

---

8. Death announcements in the newspaper and the like.

This is to publicly broadcast the death of someone. This is prohibited. At-Tirmidhī said, "Some of the scholars hate death announcements. And the death announcement in their view is to announce to the people that so and so died, so the people can witness his funeral. Some of the scholars have said there is no problem with informing a person's family and brothers."

The prohibited of death announcements has come in the narration of Hudhayfah and Ibn Mas'ūd and the meaning of the prohibition in these narrations is to go around to the people and announce the death after the person has been buried, or to announce it to those who will not pray over the person. But as for announcing the death to those who will attend the funeral and prayer over him, there is nothing wrong with this. This is based upon the narration collected in *Al-Bukhari* and *Muslim*. Abū Hurayrah ﷺ said:

أَنَّ رَسُولَ اللَّهِ صلى الله عليه وسلم نَعَى لِلنَّاسِ النَّجَاشِيَ فِي الْيَوْمِ الَّذِي مَاتَ فِيهِ فَخَرَجَ بِهِمْ إِلَى الْمُصَلَّى وَكَبَّرَ أَرْبَعَ تَكْبِيرَاتٍ.

"The Messenger of Allāh ﷺ announced the death of an-Najashi on the day he died, and he took them out to the place of prayer and observed four *takbir*."[10]

---

[10] *Ṣaḥīḥ Muslim* 951

His death was announced so the Companions could pray the funeral prayer for him because he died in a land of disbelief. And Allāh knows best.

---

9. Preventing the widow from looking at the moon and climbing on the roof, and extending the *salām* to the relatives without shaking hands.

These are some of the widespread mistakes among the common people. It has been narrated that the widow is prohibited from five permissible things during the mourning period.

1) She is prohibited from leaving her home which she lived in when her husband died except for a need or necessity.

2) She is prohibited from beautifying her clothes. Thus she leaves off beautiful clothing and wears clothes other than that.

3) She is prohibited from perfuming her clothes and body except if she does so during her menses. In this case she can do so as needed. And she does not use henna.

4) She is prohibited from wearing jewelry because this is beautification.

5) She does not use eyeliner or beautify herself with dye.

These are the five things the widow avoids during her mourning period after the death of her husband. Thus all other matters are allowed for her. She can do the permissible acts as she pleases, while having fear of Allāh and being aware that He is always observing her.

---

10. Specifying the widow with wearing black clothing.

Wearing black clothes for the widow is not mandatory. The widow is prohibited from wearing clothes with adornments during the mourning period such as bright colors or beautiful clothes. But other than this she can wear any color she pleases, black, blue, or green, as long as the garment is not beautiful such as to make her desirable. The purpose for all of this is to exalt the right of her husband and the right of their previous marriage contract. The Prophet ﷺ said:

يَحِلُّ لِامْرَأَةٍ تُؤْمِنُ بِاللَّهِ وَالْيَوْمِ الْآخِرِ أَنْ تُحِدَّ عَلَى مَيِّتٍ فَوْقَ ثَلَاثَةِ أَيَّامٍ، إِلَّا عَلَى زَوْجٍ، فَإِنَّهَا تُحِدُّ عَلَيْهِ أَرْبَعَةَ أَشْهُرٍ وَعَشْرًا، وَلَا تَكْتَحِلُ، وَلَا تَلْبَسُ ثَوْبًا مَصْبُوغًا إِلَّا ثَوْبَ عَصْبٍ، وَلَا تَمَسُّ طِيبًا إِلَّا إِذَا طَهُرَتْ، نُبْذَةً مِنْ قُسْطٍ أَوْ أَظْفَارٍ.

"It is not permissible for a woman who believes in Allāh and the last day to mourn more than three days except when mourning her husband. She mourns him for four months and ten days. (During this period) she does not use eyeliner, she does not wear dyed garments except the garment made from dyed yard. She does not wear perfume except when she becomes pure, (she can use) a piece of costus or onycha[11]."[12]

And Allāh knows best. And may the salutations of Allāh be upon our Prophet Muḥammad and upon his family and his Companions.

[11] **Translator's note:** Onycha is a type of plant used for perfume. It is call *athfar* in Arabic because it resembles a fingernail.

[12] Collected in *Al-Bukhārī* and *Muslim*.